I said to myself "I have things in my head that are not like what anyone has taught me – shapes and ideas so near to me – so natural to my way of being and thinking that it hasn't occurred to me to put them down." I decided to start anew to strip away what I had been taught....

– *Georgia O'Keeffe*

Barbara Buhler Lynes with Russell Bowman

O'Keeffe's O'Keeffes

The Artist's Collection

With 106 illustrations, 97 in colour

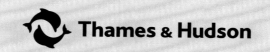

Published on the occasion of
an exhibition by the same name
originated by the Milwaukee Art
Museum and the Georgia O'Keeffe
Museum and on view in Milwaukee
from May 4 to August 19, 2001;
in Santa Fe from September 14,
2001 to January 13, 2002;
and at the Louisiana Museum
of Modern Art, Denmark from
February 8 to May 20, 2002.

First published in the United
Kingdom in 2001 by
Thames & Hudson Ltd
181A High Holborn
London WC1V 7QX

© 2001 Milwaukee Art Museum

British Library Cataloguing-in-
Publication Data
A catalogue record for this book is
available from the British Library.

ISBN: 0-500-09299-0

Coordinated and edited by
Terry Ann R. Neff,
t.a.neff associates, inc.,
Tucson, Arizona

Designed by
studio blue, Chicago

Printed and bound in Singapore
by C.S. Graphics

Frontispiece:
Myron Wood, *In the Studio*,
c. 1979/82. © Myron Wood.
Courtesy of the Pikes Peak
Library District.

Page 73:
Alfred Stieglitz, *Georgia O'Keeffe
at Lake George, August, 1818*,
1918. Courtesy of The Baltimore
Museum of Art, Gift of Cary Ross

Page 93:
Kurt Severin, *Untitled (Georgia
O'Keeffe at Work)*, c. 1930.
© K. Severin. Courtesy of Black
Star Publishers

Page 133:
Todd Webb, *Untitled (Portrait of
Georgia O'Keeffe)*, 1963.
© Todd Webb. Courtesy of the
Museum of New Mexico, Todd
Webb Study Collection

O'Keeffe Quotation Credits:
Page 1: Abraham A. Davidson,
*Early American Modernist Painting
1910–1935* (New York: Harper &
Row, 1981), pp. 63–64; p. 14:
William M. Milliken, "White Flower
by Georgia O'Keeffe," *The Bulletin
of the Cleveland Museum of
Art* 29, 4 (April 1937), p. 52;
p. 23: New York, Whitney Museum
of American Art, *Nature in
Abstraction*, text by John I. H.
Baur (New York, 1958), p. 33;
p. 24: Katharine Kuh, *The Artist's
Voice: Talks with Seventeen Artists*
(New York: Harper & Row, 1960,
1961, 1962), p. 194; p. 30:
"I Can't Sing, So I Paint! Says Ultra
Realistic Artist; Art is Not
Photography – It is Expression of
Inner Life!: Miss Georgia O'Keeffe
Explains Subjective Aspect of Her
Work," *New York Sun*, December
5, 1922, p. 22; p. 33: New York,
The Anderson Galleries, *Alfred
Stieglitz Presents One Hundred
Pictures: Oils, Water – colors,
Pastels, Drawings by Georgia
O'Keeffe, American* (New York,
1923); p. 37: Allan Keller,
"Animal Skulls Fascinate Georgia
O'Keefe [*sic*] But She Can't
Explain It – Not in Words: If She
Could She'd Have to Do It by
Painting Another Animal Skull –
New York Artist Paints Because
She Has To, But Must Be Alone,"
New York World – Telegram,
February 13, 1937, p. A2; p. 48:
Daniel Catton Rich, "The New
O'Keeffes," *Magazine of Art* 37, 3
(March 1944), pp. 110–11;
p. 51: Robert Hughes, "Loner
in the Desert," *Time*, October 12,
1970, pp. 64–67; p. 52:
Carol Taylor, "Lady Dynamo –
Miss O'Keeffe, Noted Artist,
Is a Feminist," *New York World
Telegram*, March 31, 1945,
section 2, p. 9; p. 71: B. Vladimir
Berman, "She Painted the Lily and
Got $25,000 and Fame for Doing
It! Not in a Rickety Atelier But in
a Hotel Suite on the 30th Floor,
Georgia O'Keefe [*sic*], New Find of
Art World, Sets Her Easel," *New
York Evening Graphic Magazine
Section*, May 12, 1928, p. 3M;
p. 91: Gladys Oaks, "Radical
Writer and Woman Artist Clash on
Propaganda and Its Uses – This
Is an Industrial Age, Michael Gold
Tells Georgia O'Keefe [*sic*], Who
Thinks He's All Mixed Up," *The
World*, March 16, 1930, Women's
Section, p. 1; p. 131: Charlotte
Willard, "Portrait: Georgia
O'Keeffe," *Art in America* 51, 5
(October 1963), p. 94.

Table of Contents

Preface and Acknowledgments

Georgia O'Keeffe is paradoxically one of America's best-known, yet most
enigmatic artists. The mythology that has grown up around her – her
relationship with Alfred Stieglitz, her role as "woman artist," her persona
of self-reliant individualist taking refuge in the desert – has obscured her
contributions as an artist of the very first rank. Although her first works
employing a nature-based abstraction appeared in 1915, a few years after
pioneering works by Europeans Wassily Kandinsky and Franticek
Kupka and the American Arthur Dove, both her systematic explorations
of abstraction and her compelling evocations of the natural world set
her among the most important Americans exploring this new means of
expression.

O'Keeffe is clearly one of the most prominent artists of the early twentieth
century in America, but she was also one of the first to be caught up in
the role of the artist as celebrity. Her mythology began in the 1920s when
Stieglitz exhibited his loving but highly sexualized photographic portraits of her, and continued in the Freudian reading of her works of the
1920s – 30s by Stieglitz and a number of critics. Reacting to this reading
of her abstract or highly stylized imagery (such as the close-focused
flowers), O'Keeffe increasingly sought isolation and time to work in New
Mexico. Especially after Stieglitz's death in 1946, she actively participated in the creation of her image as the austere seer of the American
Southwest: the monkishly dressed, heavily lined, but elegant figure
portrayed in photographs by Ansel Adams, Yousef Karsh, and many
others and widely distributed in books and magazines such as *Life*.

Since her death in 1986, there have been numerous visual and literary
examinations of O'Keeffe's life and her achievement as an artist, but this
exhibition signifies the first effort to illuminate the artist through an
investigation of her collection and distribution of her own work. At the
time of her death, O'Keeffe owned some 1,100 works, approximately half
of her total output. In control of her own image and marketing after
Stieglitz's death, O'Keeffe could manipulate or influence the understand-
ing of her work by what she released for sale, sent to museum exhibitions,
and allowed to be reproduced or published. Most interesting is the work
she always retained and that which she chose to distribute during her
lifetime. In 1989 The Georgia O'Keeffe Foundation was formed to handle
her estate and perpetuate knowledge of her art through gifts to museums
nationally and internationally; through publications, especially the
recently published catalogue raisonné by Barbara Buhler Lynes; the
establishment of her home in Abiquiu as a National Historic Monument;
and cooperation with a range of exhibitions and scholarly investigations.

Preface

O'Keeffe's O'Keeffes

It is fitting that the Georgia O'Keeffe Museum, which opened in 1997, and the Milwaukee Art Museum should undertake this exhibition of works from O'Keeffe's collection. The two institutions have been the primary beneficiaries of distributions from the O'Keeffe estate, through a gift/purchase arrangement with The Georgia O'Keeffe Foundation. The O'Keeffe Museum now houses sixty-two works from the estate, through the major gift/purchase supported by The Burnett Foundation and subsequent gifts and purchases. The Milwaukee Art Museum received one work as the gift of The Georgia O'Keeffe Foundation and ten additional pieces through a gift/purchase arrangement with the foundation and supported by Jane Bradley Pettit. These eleven works brought the number of pieces in the Milwaukee Art Museum to twenty-two, the fourth largest collection in the United States after those of the O'Keeffe Museum, The Metropolitan Museum of Art, and the National Gallery of Art. The concentrations of O'Keeffe's work in the O'Keeffe Museum and in the Milwaukee Art Museum are largely the result of people of exceptional vision: Anne W. Marion and John Marion, whose commitment through The Burnett Foundation both founded the museum that bears the artist's name and provided pictures to its collection; and Mrs. Harry Lynde Bradley and her daughter, Jane Bradley Pettit. Nine of the original eleven works in the Milwaukee Art Museum collection were gifts of Mrs. Bradley (and the artist graciously attended the 1975 opening of a major addition to the museum which housed the Bradley collection). The ten additional works have entered the collection through the generosity of Mrs. Pettit, who continued and expanded her mother's legacy.

Among the many individuals we must thank for the realization not only of this exhibition, but also of our collections, are Raymond R. Krueger, chair of The Georgia O'Keeffe Foundation Board, Juan Hamilton, and June O'Keeffe Sebring. As members of this board since its founding, their involvement has been central to a wider distribution of works and to the creation of the collections in Santa Fe and Milwaukee. It is fair to say that the increasing visibility of O'Keeffe estate works would not have happened without their deep belief in both the importance of O'Keeffe's work and the need for it to be more widely available to the public.

The idea for this exhibition, developed at the Milwaukee Art Museum, was prompted by the fact that O'Keeffe was a Wisconsin native and that the museum held a substantial collection. Thus, the exhibition seemed a very appropriate opening for the new Santiago Calatrava–designed Quadracci Pavilion, an addition that almost doubles the museum's size. As the largest holder of O'Keeffe estate works, the Georgia O'Keeffe

Museum was the natural partner in this endeavor. However, the execution of the exhibition is entirely the result of the knowledge and efforts of Barbara Buhler Lynes, curator of the Georgia O'Keeffe Museum and director of the Georgia O'Keeffe Museum Research Center. Her leadership and deep personal commitment to the project have been essential and her essay for this catalogue provides substantial new information and insight concerning O'Keeffe's collection.

10

We are grateful to the lenders to this exhibition, who are cited in the Acknowledgments. We would also like to thank Poul Erik Tojner, director of the Louisiana Museum of Modern Art, Denmark, for bringing this exhibition to European audiences. Our final note of deepest appreciation is to the Ameritech Foundation, which provided the largest exhibition grant the Milwaukee Art Museum has received to date, both in honor of O'Keeffe and of the museum's opening of the new addition. In Santa Fe, additional support is provided by The Burnett Foundation, the National Endowment for the Arts, New Mexico Arts, and by the City of Santa Fe Arts Commission.

Russell Bowman, *Director*
Milwaukee Art Museum

George G. King, *Director*
Georgia O'Keeffe Museum

O'Keeffe's O'Keeffes

Acknowledgments

This exhibition and its catalogue are the result of the combined efforts of many, and we would like to take this opportunity to thank those without whose help and collaboration neither could have been realized. First, we extend our thanks to the many institutions and private collectors that have generously loaned to this exhibition and provided permission to reproduce their works in the catalogue. We also are grateful for the help and support of the Board of Directors of The Georgia O'Keeffe Foundation, Anne d'Harnoncourt, Juan Hamilton, Raymond R. Krueger, Earl A. Powell III, and June O'Keeffe Sebring, and to the Foundation's Executive Director Agapita Judy Lopez, and her assistant, Ivonne Trujillo.

11

A number of museum colleagues have been extremely generous in helping us secure loans and to them we extend our thanks: at The Art Institute of Chicago, Daniel Schulman and James N. Wood; at the Brooklyn Museum of Art, Barbara Dayer Gallatti and Arnold Lehman; at The Cleveland Museum of Art, Henry Adams, Diane De Grazia, Katharine Lee Reid, and Mary Suzor; at the Dallas Museum of Art, Eleanor Jones-Harvey, John R. Lane, and Dan Rockwell; at the Iris & B. Gerald Cantor Center for Visual Arts, Stanford University, Bernard Barzyte and Thomas K. Seligman; at the Los Angeles County Museum of Art, Ilene S. Fort, Debby Freund, and Andrea L. Rich; at The Metropolitan Museum of Art, Ida Balboul, Philippe de Montebello, and Lisa Messinger; at the Musée national d'art moderne, Centre Georges Pompidou, Werner Spies; at the Museum of Fine Arts, Boston, Karen Quinn and Malcolm Rogers; at the Museum of Fine Arts, Museum of New Mexico, Sante Fe, Mary Jebsen and Joan Tafoya; at the National Museum of American Art, Fern Bleckner, Elizabeth Broun, Lynda Hartigan, and Joann Moser; at the National Gallery of Canada, Ottawa, Delphine Bishop, Pierre Théberge, and Karen Wyatt; at the National Gallery of Art, Stephanie Belt, Henry Darst, Ruth E. Fine, Carlotta Owens, Earl A. Powell III, Judith C. Walsh, and Jeffrey Weiss; at the Philadelphia Museum of Art, Anne d'Harnoncourt, Rita Gallagher, Ann B. Percy, Innis H. Shoemaker, and Ann Temkin; at The Rahr-West Art Museum, Daniel Juchniewich and Jan Smith; at the Stadische Galerie im Lenbachhaus, Helmut Friedel and Karola Rattner. Also, we would like to thank the private lenders, June O'Keeffe Sebring, Mr. and Mrs. Eugene Thaw, and three private collectors.

We are especially grateful to the many individuals at both the Georgia O'Keeffe Museum and the Milwaukee Art Museum for their various and extensive efforts on our behalf. At the Milwaukee Art Museum, we would like to acknowledge Christopher Goldsmith, executive director, for his support of this exhibition; Lucia Petrie, director of financial development, for acting as liaison to the Ameritech Foundation; Brian Ferriso, director of curatorial affairs, for development of contracts; Cyd Engel, education projects manager, for development of the exhibition's audio tour; Leigh Albritton, registrar, for shipping arrangements; and John Irion, designer, for his assistance in the design of the installation. We extend a special thank you to Marilyn Charles, executive assistant to the director, for her generous help on many aspects of the exhibition. Many other members of the Milwaukee Art Museum staff were instrumental in the programming and promotion surrounding this exhibition. John Vinci and Phil Hamp of Vinci/Hamp Architects, Chicago, provided installation plans. At the Georgia O'Keeffe Museum, we wish to thank George G. King, director, and Theresa Hays, associate director, who have given their strong support to this exhibition. We are also indebted to Lisa Arcomano, research and collections associate; Carola Clift, curatorial assistant; Marc Dorfman, director of development and special events; Ted Katsinas, director of communications; Jenni Kim, assistant to the director; Dale Kronkright, conservator; Elizabeth Martin, public relations director; Michael Shiller, assistant to the registrar, and Judy Chiba Smith, registrar. Also we wish to thank Stuart Ashman, Lamar Lynes, and Sharyn Udall.

The exhibition catalogue could not have been realized without the help and support of Terry Ann R. Neff, editor and publication manager, for whose persistence, insightful suggestions, and consistently sound advice we are especially grateful. We also want to express our appreciation for the help and support we received from the design team at studio blue, Kathy Fredrickson, Matt Simpson, and Gail Wiener. Finally, our gratitude goes to Thames & Hudson, for their patience and their belief in the project.

Barbara Buhler Lynes, *Curator*
Georgia O'Keeffe Museum,
and *The Emily Fisher Landau Director,*
Georgia O'Keeffe Museum Research Center

Russell Bowman, *Director*
Milwaukee Art Museum

Georgia O'Keeffe

Russell Bowman

An Introduction

Since her death in 1986, three biographies, a number of exhibitions, a catalogue raisonné documenting her life's work, a museum of her work founded in 1997, and many other efforts have attempted to come to terms with both the life and achievement of Georgia O'Keeffe.[1] This outpouring of critical and scholarly attention, as well as the photography books, calendars, and posters of her and her works (especially flowers) that now seem almost ubiquitous, attest to the extraordinary hold O'Keeffe has on the American imagination. Her image was built first by her husband, Alfred Stieglitz, the photographer and dealer primarily responsible for introducing modern art to American audiences, and then by O'Keeffe herself as she occasionally wrote about her work and allowed herself to be photographed at her homes in New Mexico. The image that Stieglitz built from 1916 into the 1930s of O'Keeffe as a sensual purveyor of female emotion was gradually replaced, with her increasing presence in New Mexico after 1929 and her move there in 1949, by O'Keeffe's own version of the self-reliant, austere American seer.[2] Both images have influenced but also confused her true achievement as an artist.

Only now, with the publication of the catalogue raisonné and studies of her early work and works on paper,[3] can we begin to see the unique vision and early innovation that place O'Keeffe's art among the most important by any American artist. This exhibition, which surveys the large body of work she retained (sometimes by repurchasing) in her estate at the time of her death, as well as the pictures she placed in institutions during her lifetime, seeks to illuminate the types of work she made available to the public through exhibitions, publications, and donations to institutions and that which she held in reserve, for personal reasons or perhaps because she was wary of their reception. Her collection, in any case, documents her self-awareness of her art. Surveying the sampling of pieces from her collection that comprises this exhibition, which interestingly includes most of the periods and types of work in her long career, one can begin to assess the range and power of O'Keeffe's work and her distinctive contribution to American art.

Born in Sun Prairie, Wisconsin, in 1887, O'Keeffe grew up with an appreciation for the open space of the American plains and in a family that encouraged an interest in art.[4] But strikingly she recorded in her 1976 book of personal statements and illustrations of her work, frequently from her own collection: "My first memory is of the brightness of light — light all around."[5] Works in this exhibition chosen from her collection

It is easier for me to paint it than to write about it and I would so much rather people would look at it than read about it. I see no reason for painting anything that can be put into any other form as well.

– Georgia O'Keeffe

O'Keeffe's O'Keeffes

Alfred Stieglitz, *Portrait of Georgia O'Keeffe*, 1918. Courtesy of Milwaukee Art Museum, Gift of Earl A. and Catherine V. Krueger, Jane Bradley Pettit Foundation and Friends of Art

support the idea that light – in both its formal and metaphoric aspects – forms a consistent thread and one that helps to define her achievement as an artist.[6]

O'Keeffe left the Wisconsin prairie early on – at fifteen – and pursued her study of art variously at The Art Institute of Chicago, the Art Students League in New York, and as both a student and teaching assistant to Alon Bement at the University of Virginia. Bement was a colleague of Arthur Wesley Dow at Teachers College, Columbia University, and in perhaps the most formative phase of her student years, O'Keeffe studied there with Dow in 1914–15. Dow proposed an aesthetic based on principles of Chinese and Japanese art (and the emerging style of Art Nouveau), which emphasized the arrangement of simplified, sometimes organic shapes, rather than perspectival depth. He also conveyed some ideas of his mentor, Ernest Fenollosa, whose studies of Chinese and Japanese art proclaimed a kind of Zen self-discovery. Influenced by these ideas as well as by seeing works by Rodin, Picasso, Braque, and others at Stieglitz's gallery 291, subscriptions to his publications *291* and *Camera Work*, and Wassily Kandinsky's *Concerning the Spiritual in Art*,[7] O'Keeffe was ready

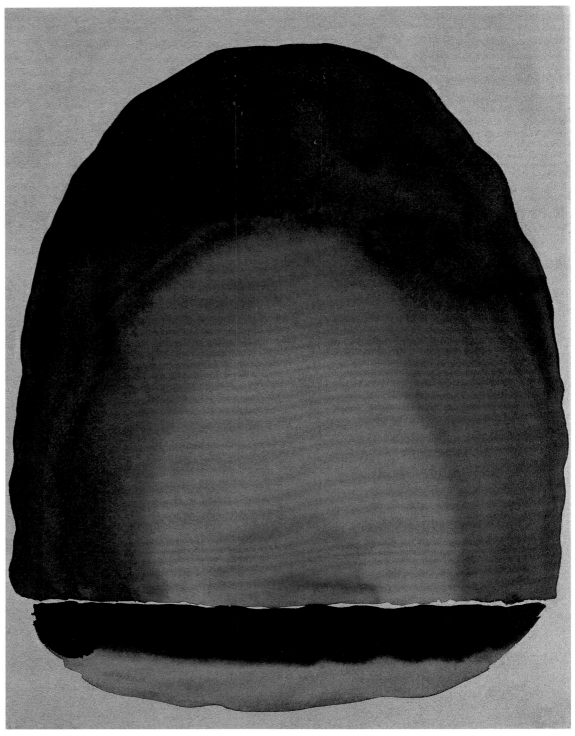

Figure 1
No. II Light Coming on the Plains, 1917
Watercolor on paper, 11 ¾ x 8 ¾ inches
Amon Carter Museum, Fort Worth, Texas
CR 210

in 1915 to seek her own way as an artist. She wrote: "It was in the fall of 1915 that I first had the idea that what I had been taught was of little value to me except for the use of materials as a language.... I decided I wasn't going to spend my life doing what had already been done."[8]

In looking at her work from the formative – and completely realized – period of 1915–18, the period before her moving to New York at Stieglitz's invitation, it becomes clear that whatever influence Stieglitz had, O'Keeffe's vision was her own. The early charcoal drawings of 1915–16 (cat. nos. 2–4), with the occasional pastel and watercolor, and even some of the works extending into 1919 reflect her wish to start at the most basic point – just black and white – and create abstract evocations of music and emotional states as advocated by Fenollosa and Kandinsky. These works represent some of the most advanced abstraction of the time, through their relative simplicity and their suggestions of a type of organic vitalism.[9] It was drawings such as these that Stieglitz so much admired and included in a group show at his gallery in 1916.

In the fall of 1916, following her first meeting with Stieglitz, O'Keeffe took a teaching position at West Texas Normal School in Canyon, Texas. Always drawn to the West, she particularly responded to its vast distances and the sense of light in a location where the sky so clearly dominates the level topography. Works such as *Sunrise and Little Clouds No. II* (1916, cat. no. 6) and *Evening Star No. VI* (1917, cat. no. 9) show her fascination not only with the spaces of the West, but with its atmospheric phenomena and light. She remarked of the Evening Star series: "We often walked away from town in the late afternoon sunset.... [I]t was like the ocean but it was wide, wide land. The evening star would be high in the sunset sky when it was still broad daylight.... I had nothing but to walk into nowhere with the wide sunset space with the star."[10] The Palo Duro Canyon series of 1916–17, done of a favorite Texas location and also evoking the time of sunset, shows O'Keeffe continuing to abstract from nature and attempting to convey her deeply felt emotional response to the scene before her. Perhaps one of her most powerful evocations of light and its meaning for her came in the 1917 series of three watercolors Light Coming on the Plains, which O'Keeffe retained in her collection until they were sold to the Amon Carter Museum, Fort Worth, at the time of her retrospective there in 1966.[11] *No. II Light Coming on the Plains* (1917, fig. 1) includes a touch of the broad plain, an arching infinitude of sky, and a tremulous glow of dawn that seem to suggest light as an almost generative force of nature. It is interesting to note, too, O'Keeffe's propensity, even in these early years, to work in series, gradually distilling both her formal means and her emotive content.

O'Keeffe's life took a radical change in 1918 with her move to New York. Not only did she begin the most pervasive personal and professional relationship of her life (Stieglitz left his wife of many years and moved in with O'Keeffe; they were married in 1924), but she also became immersed in Stieglitz's promotion of European Modernists and, more importantly, Americans who embraced the Modernist aesthetic, such as John Marin, Marsden Hartley, Arthur Dove, Charles Demuth, and the photographer Paul Strand. As their life together went on, O'Keeffe took responsibility for many of their social contacts as well as hanging many of the exhibitions in Stieglitz's successive spaces at the Anderson Galleries, the Intimate Gallery and An American Place. Immediately placed at the center of avant-garde artistic life in New York, O'Keeffe was initially stimulated and later increasingly suffocated by the aesthetic positioning and disputation of "the men."[12] Stieglitz, for his part, influenced by the Freudian theories of the time, presented her work in her first one-person show of 1917 and in succeeding years as the sensual, if not erotic, expression of the female consciousness. This sensualist reading was taken up by other critics and given a rather sensationalist reinforcement in the 1921 exhibition of Stieglitz's photographic portraits of O'Keeffe, many with a strong sensual presence, and several nude, sometimes posed suggestively against her own organically formed work. At her major exhibition of some 100 works at The Anderson Galleries in 1923 and, again with her first showing of the enlarged flowers in 1926, the sensualist, "female" reading of the works' content pervaded the critical response – a reading O'Keeffe increasingly denied.[13] However, the notoriety the artist gained through Stieglitz's photographs of her, his powerful promotion of her work, and the generally broad and positive (if, to her mind, wrong-headed) criticism of her work placed her by 1929 at the forefront of American art. She was the only woman included in the new Museum of Modern Art's "Paintings by 19 Living Americans" exhibition in 1929.

In considering the work done in New York City and during frequent visits to the Stieglitz family compound at Lake George in upstate New York, from 1918 to 1929, a dichotomy seems to emerge. The extraordinary group of oils done in 1918–20, the Series paintings (cat. nos. 17–22), and continuing into the powerful abstractions of the 1920s, are some of her most innovative works. Among those that remained in her collection were *From the Lake, No. 3* (1924, cat. no. 23), *Red, Yellow and Black Streak* of the same year (cat. no. 24), and *Grey, Blue & Black – Pink Circle* (1929, cat. no. 25). These and other works of the period continue her interest in distilling the formal and emotional essence of natural phenomena and inventing equivalents of emotional states or the power of music. They are some of the most extreme abstractions of their time in America – less dependent on natural correlatives than those by Arthur Dove, more independently invented than Stanton MacDonald-Wright's variations on Orphism or Patrick Henry Bruce's versions of Cubism – and more emotionally charged.

What is also evident, however, is that as early as 1919–20, O'Keeffe had begun to explore an alternative to these prodigious abstractions. The rather traditional still lifes of apples and shells (although *Clam Shell* [1930, cat. no. 29] is almost abstract in its focus on the interior lobes of the shell), the close-focused leaves and flowers – the latter perhaps

Josephine B. Marks, *Georgia O'Keeffe & Alfred Stieglitz, Lake George*, c. 1938. Courtesy of Sue Davidson Lowe, Madison, Connecticut

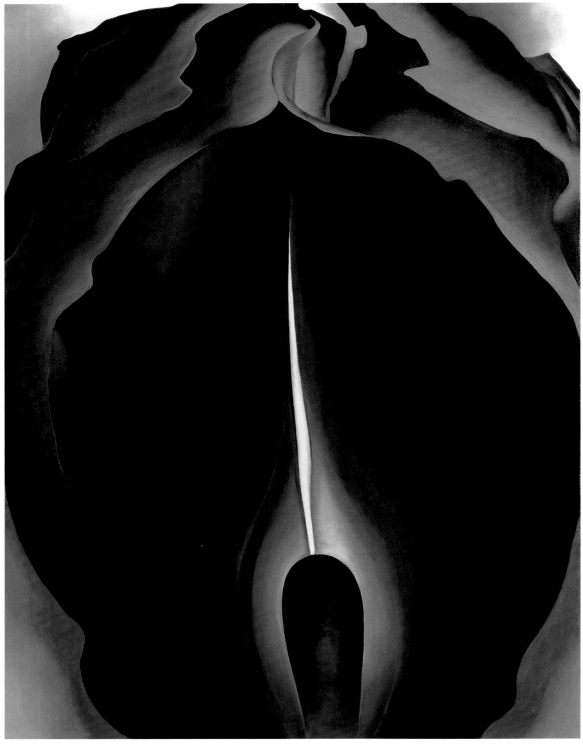

Figure 2
Jack-in-the-Pulpit No. IV, 1930
Oil on canvas, 40 x 30 inches
National Gallery of Art, Washington, DC, Alfred
Stieglitz Collection, Bequest of Georgia O'Keeffe
CR 718

influenced by the cropped photographs of Edward Steichen, Paul Strand, or Imogen Cunningham of the same period,[14] the trees and landscapes of Lake George, and the cityscapes of New York show O'Keeffe employing a more precise depiction of the motif before her. While the degree of realist detail certainly varies from highly specific in the apples and leaves to diffuse in the trees, Lake George landscapes, and the almost atmospheric *River, New York* (1928, cat. no. 41), a sense of observation of the world is palpably present. Again, it is the series works of the period that overwhelm in their development of a motif from focused realism to near complete abstraction. The Jack-in-the-Pulpit series (cat. nos. 43–45 from the series of six) demonstrates O'Keeffe moving literally into the heart of the flower, one she remembered from her early Wisconsin drawing classes.[15] And *Abstraction White Rose* (1927, cat. no. 42), certainly one of her greatest paintings, shows O'Keeffe delving into the flower's center to achieve a sense of an almost universal rhythm of growth. O'Keeffe moved between these poles of reality and abstraction, perhaps because she was wary of the early readings of her abstract imagery, but more likely because she found both to be real and necessary parts of her response to the world.

As to her treatment of light, the 1918–20 abstractions seem irradiated by a soft inner glow, a quality that continues in the subtle hues and values of works such as *Abstraction White Rose*. However, the Jack-in-the-Pulpit series shows her turning light into specific symbolic form. *Jack-in-the-Pulpit No. IV* (1930, fig. 2) shows the pistil of the flower outlined in a pure curve of light – a light form that becomes almost the entire subject of the highly abstract *Jack-in-the-Pulpit No. VI* (1930, cat. no. 45).[16] Seldom did O'Keeffe make more clear her belief in the inner vitalism of nature and her association of this force with light. The more objective works, whether still life or landscape, are bathed in an even brightness that emphasizes their outline and shape, but provides no true indication of light source or atmosphere. This relative, even light seems the correlative of the inner light of her abstractions, a kind of reflection of the indwelling spirit of objective reality. Interestingly, O'Keeffe commented about one of her Lake George paintings, *My Shanty*, the first work she sold to a public institution (1922, The Phillips Collection, Washington, DC, CR 367): "[O]ne day as I looked at the brown burned wood of the Shanty, I thought 'I can paint one of those dismal-colored paintings like the men.' I think just for fun I will try – all low-toned and dreary with the tree beside the door. In my next show, 'The Shanty' went up. The men seemed to approve of it. They seemed to think that maybe I was beginning to

Balthazar Korab, *Untitled (Georgia O'Keeffe in Her Studio)*, 1965.
© Balthazar Korab Ltd.

paint.... That was my only low-toned dismal-colored painting."[17] Beyond her obviously ironic tone about "the men," O'Keeffe's commentary points up her association of light with color and her intention to keep her paintings in a brighter-toned, more light-filled realm.

In 1929 O'Keeffe famously spent her first summer in New Mexico, which increasingly became her home. The 1930s and early 1940s were a period of increasing independence from Stieglitz, a period of growing ill health for her husband, and in 1933 an instance of physical and emotional breakdown for her, perhaps because of pressures of her planned mural for Rockefeller Center and a domestic crisis with Stieglitz.[18] In any case, she went to the Southwest desert to think, paint, and restore herself. She wrote for her exhibition catalogue at An American Place in 1939: "A red hill doesn't touch everyone's heart as it touches mine, and I suppose there is no reason it should.... All the earth colors of the painter's palette are out there in the many miles of badlands. The light naples yellow through the ochres – orange and red and purple earth – even the soft earth greens. You have no associations with those hills – our waste land – I think our most beautiful country."[19] Following Stieglitz's death in 1946 and the settlement of his estate, in 1949 O'Keeffe moved permanently to New Mexico to spend the remainder of her life there. By the 1950s and 1960s, she increasingly allowed herself to be photographed at her homes, quite consciously creating an image for herself that opposed Stieglitz's early womanly and sensualist one.[20] The image of O'Keeffe that emerged from the photographs of Ansel Adams, Yousef Karsh, and especially later, Balthazar Korab and Todd Webb – reinforced by her own paintings and writings about them – was of the independent and visionary spirit of the Southwest.

It is difficult to penetrate the mythology that O'Keeffe built around herself, but the cross section of her work from 1929 until the mid-1960s retained in her collection suggests that while the predominant Southwestern themes of architecture, still life, and landscape are continuous, their treatment underwent a basic change in the early 1940s. The works of the 1930s, both of the bones she carried back with her to New York and the New Mexico landscapes, continue the relative objectivity and the even light of the more realistic 1920s paintings. Among her masterpieces from this period are *Ranchos Church* (1929, cat. no. 49), one of a group of her earliest and most potent Southwestern subjects, and *Cow's Skull with Calico Roses* (1931, cat. no. 56), a subtle play of tones and themes of life and death. The still lifes and landscapes of the later 1930s, following her illness of 1933 and her hiatus from painting, manifest a sharp and incisive focus on the world. The landscapes particularly move from penetrating views of a single land form against a strong horizon to the slightly later, more planar, and close-focused works such as *Untitled (Red and Yellow Cliffs)* (1940, cat. no. 64) and *Cliffs Beyond Abiquiu – Dry Waterfall* (1943, cat. no. 66). It is important to note, however, that her aim was still to capture an emotive equivalent of the experience of reality. Of the 1929 *Ranchos Church*, she stated: "I long ago came to the conclusion that even if I could put down accurately the thing that I saw and enjoyed, it would not give the observer the kind of feeling it gave me. I had to create an equivalent for what I felt about what I was looking at – not copy it."[21]

In all of her subjects beginning around 1943, a transformation toward greater abstraction seems to occur. The increasingly focused view of land forms results in the Black Place series of 1943–44 in which the view of one cleft in the hills becomes almost abstract, as in *Black Place III* (1944, cat. no. 67). In still life, too, she began the Pelvis series, which reduces the view of bones to an interior one, through which one can glimpse an oval against the sky – against the light. And in the pastel *Pedernal* (1945, cat.

From experiences of one kind or another shapes and colors come to me very clearly. Sometimes I start in very realistic fashion and as I go on from one painting [to] another of the same thing, it becomes simplified till it can be nothing but abstract, but for me it is my reason for painting it, I suppose.

– Georgia O'Keeffe

no. 68), she reversed the equation to relate the sky seen through the pelvis with the infinite sky and light on the horizon. A principal subject of the 1950s, the patio of her Abiquiu house, underwent a similar transformation. A view already simplified to the point of abstraction – a well, a door, and a bit of ground or sky – the patios first deal with patterns of light and shadow and weather (cat. nos. 51–53), but in later works such as *White Patio with Red Door* (1960, fig. 3), evolve into light-filled, dazzling, near-complete abstraction. Light becomes the subject.

This direction becomes increasingly evident in the so-called "seen from an airplane" landscapes of the late 1950s and early 1960s, done following O'Keeffe's around-the-world trip and a number of other international travels. While the drawings and paintings of river beds seem to link compositionally to some of her early charcoals and watercolors of the 1915–16 period, the late paintings retained in her collection such as *Sky with Flat White Cloud* (1962, cat. no. 72) and *Winter Road I* (1963, cat. no. 73) suggest her continued absorption in issues of light. *Sky with Flat White Cloud* and the several other paintings of the subject with patterns of small clouds, culminating in her mural-scale *Sky Above Clouds IV* (1965, The Art Institute of Chicago, CR 1498), painted when she was eighty, reveal an inversion of her iconic, early Light Coming on the Plains watercolors. In *Sky with Flat White Cloud*, light irradiates the area below the horizon, suggesting an infinite, light-filled universe. In *Winter Road I*, which she based on a view from her Abiquiu bedroom window, white light obliterates all but the elegant swing of the road into the distance. O'Keeffe remarked about the two versions of this subject: "Two walls of my room in the Abiquiu house are glass and from one window I see the road toward Espanola, Santa Fe, and the world. The road fascinates me with its ups and downs and finally its wide sweep as it speeds toward the wall of my hilltop to go past me. I had made two or three snaps of it with a camera. For one of them I turned the camera at a sharp angle to get all the road. It was accidental that I made the road seem to stand up in the air, but it amused me, and I began drawing and painting it as a new shape. The trees and mesa beside it were unimportant for that painting – it was just the road."[22] Though this statement reveals her continuing commitment to conveying her emotional response to nature, the compositional principles that began with the influence of Dow, and the presence of the camera, what she does not say is that the "unimportant" parts of the landscape are subsumed by the same whiteness of light that is in some of the patio and cloud pictures of the period. These light-filled works are her last

Well, you see, we really haven't found enough dreams. We haven't dreamed enough. When you fly under even normal circumstances, you see such marvelous things, such incredible colors that you actually begin to believe in your dreams.

– Georgia O'Keeffe

O'Keeffe's O'Keeffes

Figure 3
White Patio with Red Door, 1960
Oil on canvas, 48 x 84 inches
Curtis Galleries, Minneapolis, Minnesota
CR 1445

before macular degeneration of her sight caused her to turn to assistants and to works in clay.

In surveying the works O'Keeffe retained in her collection, one sees that they touch on almost all aspects of her production and provide insight into the broad directions of her career. First, her constant attempt to capture her emotional response to nature is clear. Second, her work from its beginning in pure abstraction oscillated between poles of abstraction and representation, even elements of realism. She wrote, "It is surprising to me to see how many people separate the objective from the abstract. Objective painting is not good painting unless it is good in the abstract sense. A hill or a tree cannot make a good painting just because it is a hill or a tree. It is lines and colors put together so that they say something. For me that is the very basis of painting. The abstracted is often the most definite form for the intangible thing in myself that I can only clarify in paint."[23] In that freedom to move between aspects of reality and abstraction, between modes of representation or style, she seems like a precursor of what is now called Postmodern. Finally, it seems that there is a continuity in her pursuit of effects of light that amounts to the use of light as an informing substance, particularly in her last pictures. Light, and its correlative for her in space or distance, suggests a long tradition in American art of seeking to represent the universal or the spiritual in vast, light-filled views of nature. O'Keeffe took this tradition, beginning in the Transcendentalists and continued by the Hudson River School and a number of her Stieglitz circle colleagues such as Dove and Marin,[24] and made it entirely personal. Of an experience that seems related to *Sky with Flat White Cloud*, she wrote: "One day when I was flying back to New Mexico, the sky below was a most beautiful solid white. It looked so secure that I thought I could walk right out on it to the horizon...."[25] Whether gained from a specific reading of Transcendentalist principles, her absorption of Eastern concepts, or her own deeply felt response to the world, O'Keeffe seems to have sought a oneness with nature that she symbolized by light. From the Light Coming on the Plains watercolors to *Sky with Flat White Cloud*, her journey was consistent and complete. Both her formal innovation and her universalist content place her at the very vanguard of American art, a position her image sometimes obscures but her collection allows us to see in full.

Notes

1
For a complete bibliography, see Barbara Buhler Lynes, *Georgia O'Keeffe: Catalogue Raisonné* (New Haven and London: Yale University Press, 1999). Throughout this catalogue, "CR" refers to the catalogue raisonné number. For the purposes of this introduction, I have, with the exception of O'Keeffe's own writings, kept primarily to sources after 1986.

2
For a thorough discussion of Stieglitz's promotional and photographic image of her, his influence on critical reaction, and O'Keeffe's gradual distancing of herself from this image, see Barbara Buhler Lynes, *O'Keeffe, Stieglitz and the Critics, 1916–1929* (Ann Arbor: UMI Research Press, 1989; Chicago: University of Chicago Press, 1991). Her later image reached its broadest early public dissemination in Dorothy Seiberling, "Georgia O'Keeffe in New Mexico: Stark Visions of a Pioneeer Painter," *Life* 64 (March 1, 1968), pp. 40–50, 52–53.

3
A substantial number of early works from O'Keeffe's estate (as well as later works) were included in Jack Cowart, Juan Hamilton, and Sara Greenough, *Georgia O'Keeffe: Art and Letters* (National Gallery of Art, Washington, DC, in association with New York Graphic Society Books and Little, Brown and Company, Boston, 1987). For particular analysis of the early work on paper, see Ruth E. Fine and Barbara Buhler Lynes with Elizabeth Glassman and Judith C. Walsh, *O'Keeffe on Paper* (New York: Harry N. Abrams, 2000).

4
For a full chronology of O'Keeffe's life, see Lynes, *Catalogue Raisonné* (note 1). Excellent chronologies are also found in Charles C. Eldredge, *Georgia O'Keeffe: American and Modern* (New Haven and London: Yale University Press in association with Intercultura, Fort Worth, and Georgia O'Keeffe Foundation, 1993) and Elsa Mezvinsky Smithgall, "Georgia O'Keeffe's Life and Influences: An Illusrated Chronology," in *Georgia O'Keeffe: The Poetry of Things* (The Phillips Collection, Washington, DC, and Yale University Press in association with the Dallas Museum of Art, 1999).

5
Georgia O'Keeffe, *Georgia O'Keeffe* (New York: The Viking Press, 1976). All of the O'Keeffe statements in this essay are taken from this publication. While it is a retrospective view late in her life and undoubtedly contributed to the romanticized, Southwestern visionary image of O'Keeffe, the book also unquestionably represents how she wished to be understood.

6
Other recent studies focus on O'Keeffe's use of light, but are limited primarily to the work before 1929. See Sharyn R. Udall, *O'Keeffe and Texas* (San Antonio, Texas: Marion Koogler McNay Art Museum, 1998), pp. 45–48, and Judith Zilczer, "Light Coming on the Plains: Georgia O'Keeffe's Sunrise Series," *Artibus et Historiae* 40 (1999), pp. 191–208. My thanks to Barbara Buhler Lynes for bringing the Zilczer article to my attention.

7
Smithgall (note 4), pp. 99–101. For penetrating studies of Dow's and Fenollosa's influence, see Sarah Whitaker Peters, *Becoming O'Keeffe: The Early Years* (New York: Abbeville Press, 1991), pp. 82–93; and Elizabeth Hutton Turner, "The Real Meaning of Things," in *Georgia O'Keeffe: The Poetry of Things* (note 4), pp.1–22. For the influence of Stieglitz's shows, Kandinsky, and Eastern aesthetics, see Barbara Rose, "O'Keeffe's Originality," in Peter H. Hassrick, ed., *The Georgia O'Keeffe Museum* (New York: Harry N. Abrams, Inc. in association with the Georgia O'Keeffe Museum, 1997), pp. 99–103.

8
O'Keeffe (note 5), text accompanying plate 1.

9
For an incisive discussion of the early abstractions, see Eldredge (note 4), pp. 160–75. Although Eldridge mentions the influence of Henri Bergson's theories of *élan vital*, a more complete discussion is in Zilczer (note 6), p. 196.

10
O'Keeffe (note 5), text accompanying plate 6.

11
See Barbara Buhler Lynes, *O'Keeffe's O'Keeffes: The Artist's Collection*, p. 68, n. 32.

12
Roxanna Robinson, *Georgia O'Keeffe: A Life* (Hanover, New Hampshire: University of New England Press, 1989), pp. 245–48, 291.

13
Lynes, *O'Keeffe, Stieglitz and the Critics* (note 2), pp. 157–64.

14
Lisa Mintz Messinger, "Georgia O'Keeffe," *The Metropolitan Museum of Art Bulletin* 42, 2 (Fall 1984), p. 21.

15
O'Keeffe (note 5), text accompanying plate 41.

16
For a discussion of both the Light Coming on the Plains series and the Jack-in-the-Pulpit series in terms of light and its meaning, see Udall (note 6), pp. 45–48.

17
O'Keeffe (note 5), text accompanying plate 33.

18
For a full discussion of the Radio City Music Hall project and the O'Keeffe/Stieglitz relationship at this time, see Robinson (note 12), pp. 371–91.

19
O'Keeffe (note 5), text accompanying plates 25 and 26.

20
Stieglitz's photographs of O'Keeffe from the later 1920s and into the 1930s increasingly show her as a strong, independent, sometimes even distant woman, thus compellingly capturing the full range of her character and his response. For a full discussion of the series, see New York, The Metropolitan Museum of Art, *Georgia O'Keeffe: A Portrait by Alfred Stieglitz* (New York, 1978).

21
O'Keeffe (note 5), text accompanying plate 63.

22
Ibid., text accompanying plate 104.

23
Ibid., text accompanying plate 88.

24
For a complete discusson of O'Keeffe's relationship to Transcendentalism and American artistic traditions, see Barbara Novak, "Georgia O'Keeffe and American Intellectual and Visual Traditions," in Hassrick (note 7), pp. 73–97.

25
O'Keeffe (note 5), unpag.

O'Keeffe's
O'Keeffes

Barbara Buhler Lynes   The Artist's Collection

The art of Georgia O'Keeffe has been well known for eight decades in this country and for many years has been attaining similar prominence abroad. More than 500 examples of her works are in over 100 public collections in Asia, Europe, and North and Central America. In addition, since her work was first exhibited in New York in 1916, it has been included in hundreds of solo and group exhibitions organized around the world. Thus, it comes as something of a surprise to discover that at the time of her death in 1986, when she was ninety-eight, O'Keeffe owned more than one-half of the 2,029 known works of her total output.[1]

In her personal collection were approximately seven hundred sketches, mostly in pencil and ranging in date from 1901 to 1984; originals and casts of the three sculptures she made (in 1916, 1946, and 1982); all of her almost thirty works in clay that date from 1973 to 1984, the period she worked in this medium; approximately one hundred and fifty of the nearly four hundred works on paper she produced from 1915 to the mid-1970s; and approximately two hundred of about eight hundred oils she made between 1916 and 1976/77.[2]

The works she retained in the last two categories vary widely in both date and quality (see Appendix IV).[3] Some are obviously false starts or were left unfinished, such as *Idol* and *Idol's Head* from the 1960s. But many are at the opposite end of the spectrum, clearly among her best-known and most outstanding achievements: the watercolor *Evening Star No. VI* (1917, cat. no. 9), and the oil paintings *Red & Orange Streak / Streak* (1919, fig. 1), *Grey Line with Lavender and Yellow* (1923/24), *Abstraction White Rose* (1927, cat. no. 42), *Shell and Old Shingle IV / Shell and Old Shingle No. 4* (1926), *Jack-in-the-Pulpit No. 3* (1930, cat. no. 44), and *Black Place III* (1944, cat. no. 67). In a number about as great as the first-rate works were efforts of lesser significance, such as *Apple Family 3* (1921, cat. no. 27), *Birch and Pine Tree, No. 2* (1925, cat. no. 35), *Dark & Lavender Leaves* (1931, cat. no. 33), and *Horse's Skull with Pink Rose* (1931, cat. no. 55). Thus, O'Keeffe's collection of her own work was wide ranging in medium, date, subject matter, and quality.

The following examination of the range and significance of that collection (and in particular, of works selected from it for "O'Keeffe's O'Keeffes") and the various strategies O'Keeffe pursued in managing it, when she became its sole proprietor, demonstrates that at the same time that O'Keeffe made her living from sales during the four decades she managed her career, she also reserved examples of her work that document her

Nothing is less real than realism. Details are confusing. It is only by selection, by elimination, by emphasis, that we get at the real meaning of things.

– Georgia O'Keeffe

O'Keeffe's O'Keeffes

Figure 1
Red & Orange Streak/Streak, 1919
Oil on canvas, 27 x 23 inches
Philadelphia Museum of Art: Bequest of
Georgia O'Keeffe for the Alfred Stieglitz
Collection
CR 287

career from start to finish and stand as a testament to the complexity of her achievement. She retained works that defined her as an artist who worked on canvas or board – for which she was best known during her lifetime – and also as an artist who worked on paper supports, for which she has become increasingly well known since her death.[4]

O'Keeffe was twenty-nine in 1916 when Alfred Stieglitz included ten of her drawings in a group exhibition at his New York gallery 291. She had been making art for at least fifteen years, but this exhibition marked her debut as a serious artist. Stieglitz – almost singular in the New York art world in his willingness to support a female artist – was passionately committed to O'Keeffe's art and, from the beginning until his death in 1946, promoted her as a "woman artist." Because he had been one of this country's leading and most vocal proponents of modern art since the 1910s, his opinions carried great weight, and thus, his efforts on O'Keeffe's behalf paved the way for her ultimately establishing herself as one of this country's most important and successful artists of either gender.[5]

At the time of Stieglitz's death, when O'Keeffe took over the administration of her career, she was almost sixty. She had produced approximately three-quarters of what would be her total output, and she owned approximately two-thirds of that work. Furthermore, she had recently developed a particularly keen awareness of the body of her work. From 1944 to 1946 she had worked with Rosalind Irvine of The American Art Research Council to produce the first catalogue of her work.[6] Possibly O'Keeffe was willing to participate in this time-consuming and tedious project because she realized Stieglitz had never maintained inventories of her works or records of their sales.[7] During the three decades that he represented O'Keeffe, however, Stieglitz did document many of her exhibitions with installation photographs and checklists.[8] By using these documents, relying on O'Keeffe's memory of sales of works, and referring to the paintings Stieglitz kept in storage at An American Place (the gallery he operated from 1929 until his death), O'Keeffe and Irvine were able to catalogue more than 600 works. For every item, Irvine prepared a fact sheet listing the title, date, medium, dimensions, owner, and exhibition and publication history; for the works she was able to examine firsthand, she included the symbols or inscriptions she saw on the versos or backings.[9]

Stieglitz developed strategies to create a strong market for O'Keeffe's work. For example, as a critic pointed out in 1943: "While her paintings were ostensibly for sale, Stieglitz was loathe to part with them. The possible purchaser was hemmed about with fantastic provisos and sky-high prices. Most buyers were glad to be found worthy of acquiring an example of her art."[10] Or, as elaborated two years later by another critic: "Last week, as usual, Dealer Stieglitz was regarding prospective buyers with a critical eye. For sometimes, ownership of an O'Keeffe requires considerably more than a checkbook; the money must be accompanied by certain spiritual, emotional and intellectual qualifications satisfactory to Dealer Stieglitz."[11] Using such tactics, Stieglitz orchestrated the sale of more than 200 pictures, most of which were oils; and by the time of his death in 1946, revenues from these sales had made O'Keeffe financially independent.[12] Yet, even Stieglitz's efforts would not have been enough to sustain O'Keeffe in that she lived another forty years, and thus, the key to O'Keeffe's continuing well-being was her own management of her collection and career.

O'Keeffe had worked in oil from at least the first decade of the century and had developed a proficiency in this medium. In 1908, for example, when she was twenty-one and enrolled at the Art Students League, she received a prize for an oil painting.[13] But oil did not become her primary medium until ten years later when, at Stieglitz's invitation, she moved permanently to New York.[14] In the interim, she lived and worked in various regions of the country; and from 1915 to 1918, as she increasingly sought a personal means of expression, she worked almost exclusively in charcoal and watercolor. After that, she almost uniformly chose oil to illuminate the various ideas that interested her over the years, producing over the course of her career approximately 800 paintings.[15]

Long before Irvine began her catalogue, O'Keeffe – probably in collaboration with Stieglitz – developed a ranking system for her work. The versos and backings of many paintings are inscribed with symbols, such as five- and six-pointed stars, squares, and circles, in the middle of which O'Keeffe's initials are usually present. The meaning of this system, however, has been lost, and no comprehensive records indicate how O'Keeffe or Stieglitz priced or evaluated works.[16] But there can be no doubt that after O'Keeffe took over the management of her career, she maintained a system for ranking her work. For example, she kept records in her studio in Abiquiu, New Mexico, that documented her output, and for years she expanded and updated them. These materials, as well as letters she wrote, indicate that from time to time she reviewed and assessed her works, occasionally destroying those that did not measure up.[17] By

I found that I could say things with color and shapes that I couldn't say in any other way – things that I had no words for.

– *Georgia O'Keeffe*

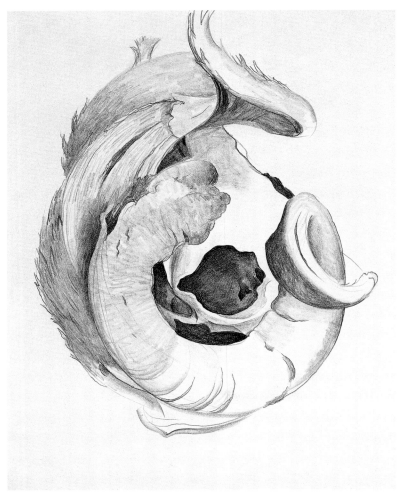

the mid-1950s, she had destroyed approximately thirty-five pictures, mostly oil paintings that ranged in date from the 1910s to the 1940s.[18] Although she never explained why she destroyed them, one can presume either that their condition had deteriorated to the point that effective restoration was not possible or that they did not in some way meet O'Keeffe's evolving standards.[19] But she did reveal aspects of her conception of quality in the various strategies she pursued as manager of her collection and career. For example, she carefully chose which works would be made available for sale or exhibition, which would be lent or given to private and public collectors, which retained, and which reacquired.

O'Keeffe's primary objective throughout her life was to be free to paint. Four years after Stieglitz's death, when she closed An American Place, O'Keeffe turned the responsibility of selling her work over to Edith Gregor Halpert, whose Downtown Gallery in New York had collaborated on a limited basis with Stieglitz since the mid-1930s. During the thirteen years that Halpert represented O'Keeffe (1950–63), The Downtown Gallery handled approximately three hundred and fifty works, which represented about half of O'Keeffe's output to 1963. These works were consigned either from storage in New York or shipped by O'Keeffe from New Mexico. In New York, Doris Bry, who began working for O'Keeffe in 1946, served as liaison with Halpert.

Although O'Keeffe was living in New Mexico during the years that she was represented by The Downtown Gallery, she worked hand-in-hand with Halpert to make decisions about the nature of her exhibitions and to establish prices for her work. Halpert maintained extensive consignment, exhibitions, price, and sales records for the works she received from O'Keeffe; and because some works were consigned more than once in this period, the records document their escalating values.[20] Prices of O'Keeffes for sale over the years at The Downtown Gallery ranged from $150 to $12,000. Of the sixteen works in charcoal that Halpert handled, some were available at $150, such as *Goat's Horns II* (1945, fig. 2), while others, such as *Drawing V* (1959, cat. no. 70), were valued at $1,000. For the approximately sixty watercolors that O'Keeffe consigned to Halpert, prices varied from $500 (*Morning Sky with Houses* [1916, cat. no. 7]) to $800 (*Sunrise and Little Clouds No. II* [1916, cat. no. 6]). O'Keeffe placed about sixteen pastels with Halpert and priced them from $500 (*No. 32 – Special* [1915, cat. no. 1]) to $6,000 (*An Orchid* [1941, fig. 3]). The approximately 250 consigned oil paintings varied in price from $250 (*Squash Blossoms* [1925, private collection, CR 498]) to $12,000 (*2 Calla Lilies on Pink* [1928, cat. no. 47], *It Was Blue and Green* [1960], and *It Was Yellow and Pink III* [1960, cat. no. 71]).

Two consigned works were marked "Not For Sale": *Red & Orange Streak / Streak* and *Shell & Old Shingle II / Shell and Old Shingle No. II* (1926), one of a series of seven paintings of this subject. Though exhibited, these works were withheld from the market by O'Keeffe either because she could not determine a price for them or because she was keenly aware of their importance to her work as a whole and, like Stieglitz, did not wish to part with them.[21] Whatever the case, they remained in her collection until her death in 1986, as did some of those that had been available for sale at The Downtown Gallery: *Drawing V*, *Sunrise and Little Clouds No. II*, *No. 32 – Special*, *An Orchid*, *2 Calla Lilies on Pink*, and *It Was Yellow and Pink III*. Many of these are now considered among O'Keeffe's best single or series paintings.

Figure 3
An Orchid, 1941
Pastel on paper mounted on cardboard
27 5/8 x 21 3/4 inches
The Museum of Modern Art, New York,
Bequest of Georgia O'Keeffe
CR 1017

O'Keeffe's and Halpert's system for assigning prices to works was probably based on various criteria, such as subject matter, date, medium, and size. In fact, in many ways, it seems quite arbitrary and reflective of O'Keeffe's personal feelings about particular works. But works priced identically in Halpert's lists vary so dramatically in each of these areas that it is impossible to determine the mechanisms of their system. For example, there were seven works priced at $8,000, ranging in date from 1926 to 1959 and in size from 30-by-36 to 48-by-30 inches, such as the oils *City Night* (1926, fig. 4) and *Blue B* (1959, fig. 5).[22] These works also vary widely in subject.

In a more modest price category, ten works were for sale at $800, including eight watercolors and two oils. They include the four watercolors titled *Blue (Nos. I–IV)* (1916, figs. 6A and 6B), the smaller watercolor *Starlight Night* (1917), and the 20-by-36-inch oil *Grey Hills Painted Red* (1930, fig. 7).[23] But curiously, the watercolor *Canyon with Crows* (1917), clearly of a quality comparable to those listed at $800 and equal in size to *Starlight Night,* was priced at $500. And seven watercolors from the Evening Star series, which are the same size as *Starlight Night* and represent some of O'Keeffe's most important works in this medium, were priced at $600. It is interesting that at her death O'Keeffe owned two works from the Evening Star series and all of the other watercolors mentioned above, with the exception of *Blue (Nos. I–IV)*. She must have known early on that these works were among her most outstanding watercolors, as she kept them for herself for nearly seventy years.

Similar discontinuities in valuation characterize other works O'Keeffe consigned to Halpert. *Inside Red Canna* (1919, fig. 8), which measures 22-by-17 inches, is one of O'Keeffe's earliest depictions of flowers as if seen close up. In spite of its importance in this regard, it was priced at $500, while a somewhat smaller oil, *A Sunflower from Maggie* (1937, cat. no. 48), was priced at $7,000. Similarly, the oil *Nature Forms – Gaspé* (1932) measuring 10-by-24 inches and one of O'Keeffe finest abstractions, was priced at $3,000. This figure was also assigned to the much larger oil (30 x 16 inches) *Thigh Bone on Black Stripe* (1931, fig. 9), as well as to an oil of landscape subject matter (16 x 36 inches), *Abiquiu Sand Hills and Mesa* (1944/45, fig. 10). But the oil *Corn, No. 2* (1924, cat. no. 38), measuring 27-by-10 inches, was priced at $5,000. At $7,000, *A Sunflower from Maggie,* whose title refers to Margaret Johnson, one of O'Keeffe's friends, was equal in price to several much larger oils, including *Deer's Skull with Pedernal* (1936, fig. 11), *Horse's Skull with Pink Rose,* and *Only*

My pictures are my statement of a personal experience.... People like them, if they do, because they are colorful, but they are disturbed because they cannot interpret them.

– *Georgia O'Keeffe*

Figure 4
City Night, 1926
Oil on canvas, 48 x 30 inches
The Minneapolis Institute of Arts,
Minneapolis, Minnesota, Gift of the Regis
Corporation, Mr. and Mrs. W. John Driscoll,
The Beim Foundation, the Larsen Fund, and
by public subscription
CR 529

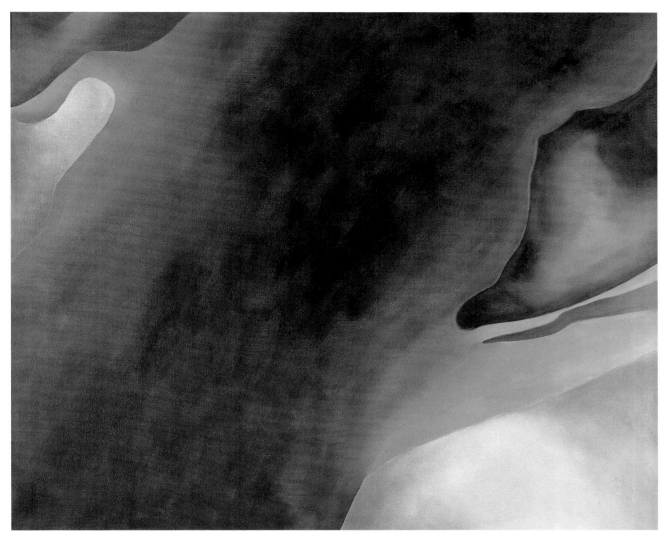

Figure 5
Blue B, 1959
Oil on canvas, 30 x 36 inches
Milwaukee Art Museum, Milwaukee,
Wisconsin, Gift of Mrs. Harry Lynde Bradley
CR 1357

Figure 6A
Blue No. II, 1916
Japanese gampi
One of four sheets, each 15 7/8 x 11 inches
Brooklyn Museum of Art, New York,
Bequest of Mary T. Cockcroft and Dick S.
Ramsay Fund
CR 92

One (1959, fig. 12); but it is hardly comparable to them in importance. As with *Corn, No. 2,* which depicts plants from O'Keeffe's garden at Lake George that obviously meant a great deal to her, *A Sunflower from Maggie* must have been particularly meaningful, indicating that the prices she established were not always commensurate with quality. Apparently, although O'Keeffe was willing to make such paintings available for sale, she was willing to part with them only if their sales generated significant income.

Considering her already solid financial footing, which allowed O'Keeffe ample opportunity to be somewhat manipulative about the availability and pricing of her work, revenues received from the approximately 200 works she allowed Halpert to see over the years provided more than sufficient income for the artist, which made it possible for O'Keeffe to remain financially secure. Moreover, Halpert helped her sustain the position of prominence she had enjoyed since the 1920s. She exhibited O'Keeffe's works regularly in group exhibitions at The Downtown Gallery; she staged three solo exhibitions of O'Keeffe's work at the gallery (which O'Keeffe orchestrated and installed); she loaned many works to important national and international group exhibitions; and she assisted O'Keeffe with the 1960 retrospective exhibition of her work at the Worcester Art Museum in Massachusetts.[24] When their business relationship ended in 1963, Halpert returned to O'Keeffe approximately 150 works that she had in inventory, many of which went back into storage in New York.[25] Ninety-two of these works subsequently remained with O'Keeffe and were in her collection at the time of her death.[26]

Approximately 200 additional works were sold between 1963 and 1984, either by Doris Bry, who worked as O'Keeffe's agent from 1963 to 1977, or by O'Keeffe herself after 1977. Some were among the approximately 238 works O'Keeffe had produced since 1946, when she and Irvine completed the first catalogue of her work. But after her relationship with Halpert ended, no subsequent list of all the works in O'Keeffe's collection with assigned specific values has been discovered.[27] Thus, Halpert's pricing records, despite their seeming anomalies, are particularly important: they function as an index to the values once assigned to nearly one-quarter of the 350 oils, watercolors, and finished drawings that never again left O'Keeffe's collection.

Access to O'Keeffe's work became increasingly difficult after Halpert and O'Keeffe parted ways. First, the work was no longer available

Figure 6B
Blue No. III, 1916
Japanese gampi
One of four sheets, each 15 ⅞ x 11 inches
Brooklyn Museum of Art, New York,
Bequest of Mary T. Cockcroft and Dick S.
Ramsay Fund
CR 93

at a New York gallery; and second, only O'Keeffe's closest associates had access to the records she kept in New Mexico.[28] Thus, although O'Keeffe made a limited amount of her work available to selected buyers through Bry, after Bry ceased to function as her agent in 1977, O'Keeffe alone knew the extent of what she owned.[29] Through publications, however, O'Keeffe did identify a substantial number of the works that she retained in her collection. First, there are the checklists she prepared for the last three retrospective exhibitions of her work that took place before her death: in addition to the Worcester show (1960), those held at the Amon Carter Museum, Fort Worth, Texas (1966) and the Whitney Museum of American Art, New York (1970).[30] O'Keeffe assumed complete control over these exhibitions, even supervising their installations (see Appendix I).[31]

It is obvious from the catalogue she helped Irvine assemble in the 1940s that O'Keeffe knew the whereabouts of hundreds of works that had been sold over the years. But only eleven of the forty-three pictures she selected for the Worcester exhibition came from public and private collections; O'Keeffe loaned the remaining thirty-two. Similarly, she loaned forty-nine of the one hundred and fourteen works selected for the Amon Carter show and fifty-eight of the one hundred and twenty-one selected for the Whitney show. Of the total one hundred and sixty-nine individual works included in these exhibitions (many appeared in at least two),

Figure 7
Grey Hills Painted Red, 1930
Oil on canvas, 20 x 36 inches
Private collection, Winnetka, Illinois
CR 729

Figure 8
Inside Red Canna, 1919
Oil on canvas, 22 x 17 inches
Michael and Fiona Scharf, New York
CR 306

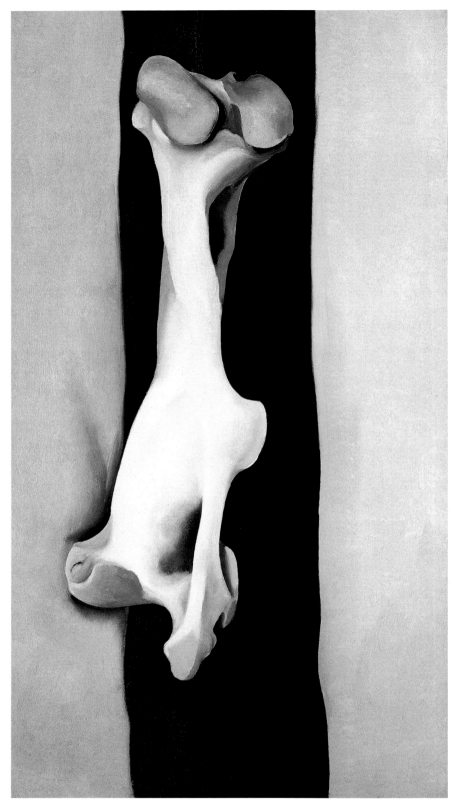

Figure 9
Thigh Bone on Black Stripe, 1931
Oil on canvas, 30 x 16 inches
Private collection, Cleveland
CR 778

O'Keeffe owned one hundred and six. Most had not been seen since they were first exhibited by Stieglitz and, because they had never been consigned to Halpert, had not been known for decades. A few had been completed after 1963 and, thus, were being exhibited for the first time.

The range of works O'Keeffe selected for these exhibitions is interesting. For example, in the Worcester show, she exhibited works of the highest quality, such as *Red & Orange Streak / Streak*, which she would ultimately name among her bequests to institutions, and *Pelvis Series, Red with Yellow* (1945), which was sold by the artist directly in 1963. But she also exhibited works of lesser importance, such as *Seaweed* (1927, cat. no. 30), which was in her collection at her death, and *Purple Hills* (1935), which was sold to a private collector in 1971. Such variations characterize her selection of works for each of the retrospective exhibitions. Clearly, she believed every work she selected worthy of inclusion in a major museum exhibition, but it is just as clear that some works were selected in anticipation of sales.[32]

Two oil paintings shown for the first time in the Worcester exhibition were sold shortly thereafter to private collectors: *It Was Red and Pink* (1959) and *It Was Blue and Green*. The Amon Carter exhibition was directly responsible for the sales of six works, also to private collectors: *Evening Star No. V* (1917), *Open Clam Shell* (1926), *Closed Clam Shell* (1926), *My Heart* (1944), *Red Hills and Sky* (1945), and *Sky Above Clouds III / Above the Clouds III* (1963). Of the works shown in the Whitney exhibition, in

Figure 10
Abiquiu Sand Hills and Mesa, 1944/45
Oil on canvas, 16 x 36 inches
Private collection, New York
CR 1085

Figure 11
Deer's Skull with Pedernal, 1936
Oil on canvas, 36 x 30 inches
Museum of Fine Arts, Boston, Gift of
the William H. Lane Foundation
CR 879

Figure 12
Only One, 1959
Oil on canvas, 36 x 30 inches
National Museum of American Art,
Smithsonian Institution, Washington, DC,
Gift of S.C. Johnson & Son, Inc.
CR 1359

Eliot Porter, *Georgia O'Keeffe and Head by Mary Callery, Ghost Ranch, New Mexico*, 1945. © 1990 and courtesy of Amon Carter Museum, Fort Worth, Texas, Bequest of Eliot Porter

I have used these things to say what is to me the wideness and wonder of the world as I live in it.

– Georgia O'Keeffe

1971 private collectors bought three oils: *Grey Lines with Black, Blue and Yellow* (1923/25), *Purple Hills*, and *Sky Above Clouds II* (1963); the San Diego Museum of Art purchased *The White Flower* (1932).[33] And between 1972 and 1974, private collectors bought three additional oils seen in this exhibition: *Music – Pink and Blue No. I* (1918), *59th St. Studio* (1919), and *Black Place Green* (1949). The works that sold primarily as a result of their inclusion in these three exhibitions represent a broad response to O'Keeffe's art both in terms of date and subject matter. They were made in each of the seven decades of her activity to that point, and they represent image concerns for which O'Keeffe had become best known over the years, including both representational subject matter and abstraction.

Sixty-six of the works included in these retrospective exhibitions were in O'Keeffe's collection in 1986. It is tempting to say that they remained with her over the years because they had not attracted buyers, but there is evidence to suggest that O'Keeffe may have kept some of these works for herself because she thought they were particularly important examples of her work.[34] Eight were included in all of her retrospectives: *From the Lake, No. 3* (1924, cat. no. 23), two of the Shell and Old Shingle paintings (1926), *Abstraction White Rose, Seaweed, Cliffs Beyond Abiquiu –*

O'Keeffe's O'Keeffes

Dry Waterfall (1943, cat. no. 65), *Black Place III*, and *Pelvis IV* (1944, cat. no. 59). Moreover, five of the eight were among the one hundred and twenty-eight works reproduced as illustrations for the two books O'Keeffe published in the 1970s about her art and life: *Some Memories of Drawings* (1974), and *Georgia O'Keeffe* (1976).[35] These included the two Shell and Old Shingle paintings, *Cliffs Beyond Abiquiu – Dry Waterfall*, and *Black Place III*.

Approximately one-third of the images in these books describe works that had been included in the retrospective exhibitions and remained in O'Keeffe's collection, but O'Keeffe also illustrated fourteen paintings and six drawings that had not previously been identified as belonging to her, thus increasing public awareness of its extent.[36] The works reproduced in these publications, like those selected for her retrospectives, were drawn from each of the seven decades O'Keeffe had been active as an artist and were among those she obviously felt best represented what she had set out to achieve. As she suggested in her discussion of the Shell and Old Shingle series in *Georgia O'Keeffe:* "I find that I have painted my life – things happening in my life." Or, in discussing the Black Place, which inspired three works reproduced in her publications, she pointed out: "I must have seen the Black Place first driving past on a trip into the Navajo country [1936] and, having seen it, I had to go back to paint [1941–45] – even in the heat of mid-summer. It became one of my favorite places to work...."[37] Clearly, the pictures O'Keeffe chose to include in these books had meaning for her beyond the objects themselves. In fact, of the one hundred and eighty-nine works O'Keeffe selected for her retrospective exhibitions and these publications, she owned eighty-three at her death.

O'Keeffe's publications reinforced the renewed public awareness of her and her art that occurred after the Whitney show – approximately half a century after Stieglitz had first staged major shows of her work in New York.[38] In addition, in the 1970s, O'Keeffe became increasingly willing to entertain requests for interviews and allowed herself to be photographed for many publications.[39] In 1977 she participated in the making of *Georgia O'Keeffe*, the Perry Miller Adato film about her art and life that was aired on National Public Television in November 1978.

In short, after over thirty years of managing her own career, the artist became even more widely known than she had been during the thirty years that Stieglitz managed it. Moreover, increasingly in interviews in the 1970s and 1980s, O'Keeffe was careful to characterize herself as a loner and pioneer, whose success as an artist had been dependent on a commitment to hard work and the self-imposed isolation of her life in the Northern New Mexico desert. O'Keeffe's characterization of herself as a self-realized, hard-working individualist differed dramatically from the way Stieglitz had promoted her from the moment he first saw her work in 1916: as a liberated woman whose art was an unconscious manifestation of her sexuality.[40]

50

In fact, during the forty years that O'Keeffe was in charge of promoting herself, she referred less and less frequently to Stieglitz and the role he had played in her success. In *Some Memories of Drawings*, for example, she makes no reference to him; in *Georgia O'Keeffe*, his name appears only once.[41] Moreover, beginning in the 1970s, she actively disassociated herself from feminist artists and art historians, who had credited O'Keeffe as the originator of female iconography by describing her work – particularly her flower paintings – in essentialist terms that resembled those Stieglitz had used when promoting O'Keeffe's early abstractions in the 1910s and early 1920s.[42] Thus, in the last decades of her life, O'Keeffe finally was able to define herself in her own way and on her own terms.

As early as 1947, O'Keeffe began distributing works to institutions as a management strategy to offset taxes from earnings on sales. Between then and 1984, she gave twenty-three pictures to the Carl Van Vechten Museum of Art, Fisk University, Nashville, Tennessee; The Metropolitan Museum of Art, New York; The Art Institute of Chicago; and the Philadelphia Museum of Art (see Appendix II). These gifts represented her work from the 1910s to the 1960s and included several signature pieces, such as *Black Iris* (1926), *Ranchos Church* (1930, cat. no. 50), *Clam Shell* (1930, cat. no. 29), *Cow's Skull, Red, White and Blue* (1931), and *Cow's Skull with Calico Roses* (1931, cat. no. 56). Other works among these gifts could be considered of lesser importance, such as *Corn Dark* (1924), *Shell, No. I* (1928), *River, New York* (1928, cat. no. 41), *A Sunflower from Maggie, Red and Pink Rocks and Teeth* (1938), and *Flying Backbone* (1944). But *Shell, No. I, River, New York*, and *A Sunflower from Maggie* – regardless of how their relative importance to her work may be interpreted today – apparently meant a great deal to O'Keeffe: they were among many works that she repurchased or traded back over the years.

In fact, from 1947 to 1983, at least seventy-five works that left O'Keeffe's collection through gifts, sales, and trades, were reacquired by the artist.

O'Keeffe's O'Keeffes

They range in date from the 1910s through the 1950s and represent the broad range of O'Keeffe's interests as a painter. Among these are: *No. 32 – Special, Morning Sky with Houses, Calla Lily – Tall Glass – No. 1* (1923, private collection, CR 425), *City Night, Small Purple Hills* (1934, cat. no. 61), *Ram's Skull with Brown Leaves* (1936, Roswell Museum and Art Center, Roswell, New Mexico, CR 881) and *Black Door with Snow* (1955, cat. no. 53). Although it is not clear why O'Keeffe wanted possession of each of these works, it is possible that she reacquired some of them to maintain her broad market valuation, especially in the cases of those that became available at auction. That she recognized the importance of maintaining her price structure is clear from a letter she wrote in 1947 to Albert C. Barnes, who had expressed interest in her work: "There are certain pictures of mine that Stieglitz had asked high prices for and because so many people have said he was crazy to have such ideas I have wanted to remove those things from the market so that no one would get them for less than he asked."[43] Thus, by repurchasing her work – particularly at auction – she could control public perception of its value, an action that implicitly demonstrated her belief in the price structure Stieglitz had established.

O'Keeffe resold some of the works she reacquired over the years, most probably because she was able to obtain the price she felt their value demanded. These include: *Petunia and Coleus* (1924, private collection, CR 463), *City Night*, and *Red Barn* (1928, private collection, CR 618). But overall, she kept more than half of the works she reacquired, which implies that she was interested in them primarily because they were important to her personally or to the body of her work. Support for this interpretation comes, in part, from a rare 1977 comment about what one of the works she repurchased, *No. 32 – Special*, meant to her. About this work and a similar pastel she completed in 1915, O'Keeffe stated: "These abstractions were done after sitting on the edge of a river, and having a conversation with a friend about abstractions from nature. I went home and made two pastels to illustrate to him what I meant." Much earlier, in a letter, she had referred to these works more specifically as portraits: "[This] is Political Science [Arthur Whittier Macmahon] and me – dabbling our feet in the water – It is about fifteen feet deep right under our feet – is red from the red clay."[44] Clearly, the pastels were important to O'Keeffe because of her friendship with Macmahon and because of the idea implicit in them that experience could be expressed through abstraction.

Sometimes I have resisted painting something that seemed to me so ordinary, hardly worth doing. But when I do it and it's done, it's different from what other people see. It is ordinary to me, but not to you.

– Georgia O'Keeffe

O'Keeffe also tried to reunite individual pictures from three remarkable series. By 1973, with the repurchase of *Jack-in-the-Pulpit, No. 4* (see Bowman, fig. 2), O'Keeffe owned all but one of the six paintings from this major series dating from 1930. The fact that four had remained with her since their completion in itself indicates that she felt the series was important.[45] But she had also included five of the paintings in the Whitney retrospective as well as in *Georgia O'Keeffe*, where she explained how she had made them: "The year I painted them I had gone to the lake early in March. Remembering the art lessons of my high school days [when she had also painted this flower], I looked at the Jacks with great interest. I did a set of six paintings of them. The first painting was very realistic. The last one had only the Jack from the flower."[46]

Also in the Whitney exhibition, O'Keeffe exhibited five works from the Shell and Old Shingle series that she had kept with her since painting them in 1926, along with *Shell and Old Shingle VI*, which had been sold in 1929. She had tried repeatedly in the late 1960s to reacquire *VI*; and although her efforts were not successful, they document her determination to try to reunite it with the others from the series that she owned.[47]

The Evening Star watercolor series also meant a great deal to O'Keeffe, as is clear from her description of its inspiration in *Georgia O'Keeffe:* "The evening star would be high in the sunset sky when it was still broad daylight. That evening star fascinated me. It was in some way very exciting to me.... I had nothing but to walk into nowhere and the wide sunset space with the star."[48] She had owned *Evening Star No. IV* since creating it in Texas in 1917 and repurchased *Evening Star No. VI* when the opportunity presented itself in 1971.

That O'Keeffe recognized the significance of her early watercolors was clear as early as 1958, when she included fifty-three of them in an exhibition she organized at The Downtown Gallery. In 1963, when Halpert returned the ones remaining at the gallery, she marked twelve of them "Not For Sale," including two of the Evening Star watercolors ultimately sold. And in 1969, as she was organizing work for the Whitney retrospective, she pointed out in reference to her early drawings and watercolors: "We don't really need to have the show, I never did any better."[49] Thus, in buying back one of the Evening Star watercolors in 1971, O'Keeffe reinforced her belief in the importance of her early works on paper to the whole of her output.

It's the most wonderful place you can imagine.... It's so beautiful there. It's ridiculous. In front of my house there are low scrub brushes and cottonwood trees and, further out, a line of hills. And then I have this mountain. A flat top mountain that slopes off on each side. A blue mountain. And to the left you can see snow covered mountains, far, far away.

– Georgia O'Keeffe

O'Keeffe's O'Keeffes

Balthazar Korab, *Untitled (Georgia O'Keeffe at Home)*, 1965.
© Balthazar Korab Ltd. Courtesy of B. Korab

Toward the end of the 1970s, O'Keeffe signed a will in which she named fifty-two works as bequests to seven institutions: The Art Institute of Chicago; the Brooklyn Museum of Art; The Cleveland Museum of Art; The Metropolitan Museum of Art and The Museum of Modern Art, New York; the Philadelphia Museum of Art; and the National Gallery of Art, Washington, DC (see Appendix III). Her bequests included thirteen works that she had not previously publicized as belonging to her and thirty-eight that had been publicized as such in either her retrospectives or her books. Of these, she specifically named four pictures that she had included in all of her retrospectives: *From the Lake, No. 3*, two of the Shell and Old Shingle paintings (1926), and *Cliffs Beyond Abiquiu – Dry Waterfall*.

But she included among her bequests neither *Evening Star No. VI* nor many of the other works she reacquired over the years. Moreover, the bequests did not include thirty-five of the works that she had selected for her books or retrospectives. Why she did not specify the disposition of works she clearly felt were important is not clear. In fact, she left to the executor of her estate the responsibility of distributing everything remaining in her collection, which included approximately sixty three-dimensional works, over two hundred and eighty-five finished paintings and drawings, and seven hundred essentially unknown sketches. This situation recalls what Stieglitz had done in 1946, when he left the distribution of his entire collection of paintings and photographs to O'Keeffe. One could assume that O'Keeffe did not consider the unknown works in her collection in the same category as those she had made public or named as bequests.

Certainly this is true of the sketches, which are largely important only in that they reveal a relatively unknown dimension of O'Keeffe's working methods – a lifelong habit of making preparatory drawings for works in other mediums.[50] Over the years she gave a few sketches to friends and close associates, and in the 1980s, a handful of these began to be included in exhibitions of her work and reproduced in exhibition catalogues, but she rarely referred to this aspect of her activity.[51] She stored many of them systematically in manila folders that she labeled with words such as "Rivers," demonstrating that they had been important enough to her to organize and file by subject.[52] But among them are large numbers of single drawings dating from the 1920s through the 1960s that relate directly to specific, well-known paintings. There is *Untitled (New York Street with Moon)* (1925, cat. no. 40) for *New York Street with Moon* (1925, fig. 13), *Ranchos Church* (1929, cat. no. 49), a preparatory drawing for the series of paintings O'Keeffe completed of this structure, such as *Ranchos Church* (1930, cat. no. 50), and *Horse's Skull with Pink Rose* (1931, cat. no. 54) for *Horse's Skull with Pink Rose* (cat. no. 55).

In all probability, O'Keeffe made numerous preparatory sketches for each of these works, as she had done in 1916–17, when she made more than twenty pencil sketches of the Palo Duro Canyon before experimenting with this subject in charcoal and oil, producing, among other works, *Untitled (Palo Duro Canyon Landscape)* (1916/17, cat. nos. 11–14), *No. 15 Special* (1916/17, fig. 14), and *No. 21 – Special* (1916/17, cat. no. 16). Thus, it seems likely that she edited her sketches, just as she had edited her paintings, retaining only those that were of particular importance to her.

Many of the approximately 250 unknown finished works in O'Keeffe's collection at her death, however, are as high in quality as many of the ones

Figure 13
New York Street with Moon, 1925
Oil on canvas mounted to masonite
48 x 30 inches
Carmen Thyssen-Bornemisza Collection,
Lugano, Switzerland
CR 483

Figure 14
No. 15 Special, 1916/17
Charcoal on laid paper, 18 ⅞ x 24 ⅜ inches
Philadelphia Museum of Art: Purchased
with the gift (by exchange) of Dr. and
Mrs. Paul Todd Makler, funds contributed
by Mr. and Mrs. John J. F. Sherrerd, and
gift of The Georgia O'Keeffe Foundation
CR 154

she had acknowledged as in her collection. As might be expected, they represent a broad range of her abstract and representational work, including *Nude Series* (1917, cat. no. 8), *Series I, No. 8* (1919, cat. no. 21), *Apple Family – 2* (1920, cat. no. 26), *Petunias* (1925, fig. 15), *Canna Leaves* (1925, cat. no. 31), *Tan Clam Shell with Seaweed* (1926, cat. no. 28), *Turkey Feathers in Indian Pot* (1935, cat. no. 57), *The Cliff Chimneys* (1937, cat. no. 63), *In the Patio VIII* (1950, cat. no. 51), *Another Drawing Similar Shape* (1959, cat. no. 69), and *Sky with Flat White Cloud* (1962, cat. no. 72).

It is astonishing that nearly one-third of the works O'Keeffe owned at her death were produced during the first seven of the more than eighty years of her mature career; that is, between 1915 and 1922. Moreover, more than half of these early works were abstractions, many of which had not been seen since they were exhibited in 1916, 1917, or 1923. O'Keeffe may have kept such a significant number of her early abstractions out of the public eye because she knew that abstraction, as a means of expression, did not have as strong a market as her more representational work. Yet she seems to have kept private specific works she had made between 1915 and 1922 as part of her management strategies.

In 1915 O'Keeffe was an unknown artist teaching at Columbia College, Columbia, South Carolina. By January 1923 she had become something entirely different – a well-known artist whose work was being exhibited in New York. The beginning of this dramatic shift of fortune came about in the fall of 1915, when in an attempt to discover a means of expression that was entirely her own, she abandoned imitative realism, which had formed the basis of her earlier training, to commit herself to the language of abstraction. She subsequently produced a series of drawings that are among the most innovative in all of American art of this period and that soon brought her to the attention of Stieglitz. He was enthusiastic about her charcoal abstractions from the moment he first saw them in January 1916, and he exhibited some of them the following May.

These works clearly were important to O'Keeffe: at her death, she owned all of the known charcoal abstractions she made in 1915, with the exception of *No. 9 Special* (1915, fig. 16), which had been sold the year before she died. These include *No. 20 – From Music – Special* (1915, cat. no. 2), *Early Abstraction* (1915, cat. no. 3), and *No. 14 Special* (1915). She not only retained these charcoal abstractions for more than seventy years, but, after she began to supervise her own career, also had kept all but one other out of the public eye: *No. 12 – Special* (1915).[53]

This is also true for nearly half of the twenty-three works that O'Keeffe completed between May 1916 and early 1917 that Stieglitz included in the one-person exhibition of her work he organized in 1917. These included one sculpture, six charcoals (one now lost), ten watercolors (one now lost), and six oils. Nearly every work in the exhibition was abstract, and in 1986 O'Keeffe owned ten of the twenty-one known works it had included, among them, *Sunrise and Little Clouds No. II*, *No. 12 Special* (1916), and *No. 20 – Special* (1916/17, cat. no. 15). During her lifetime, moreover, O'Keeffe publicized only three of the ten she owned: *No. 15 Special* (1915), *No. 21 – Special* (1916/17), and *No. 22 – Special* (1916/17).

58

Between 1915 and 1918, when she moved from Texas to New York, O'Keeffe worked primarily on paper. But after her move to New York, she began working primarily in oil, most probably as a result of Stieglitz's encouragement; for although he believed that O'Keeffe's works on paper were important, he also knew that in order for her to be taken seriously as an artist in New York, she had to demonstrate proficiency in oil.[54]

Of the approximately 328 works O'Keeffe had completed since 1915, Stieglitz included over 100 in the next exhibition of her work that opened in January 1923. More than half of the works in this exhibition demonstrated her continuing experiments with abstraction either on canvas or paper. In fact, her most provocative and distinctive early abstractions in oil were completed in and after 1918, *Music – Pink and Blue No. I*, *Series I – No. 2* (1918, cat. no. 17), *Series I – No. 3* (1918, cat. no. 18), *Series I, No. 4* (1918, cat. no. 19), *Series I – From the Plains* (1919, fig. 17), *Series I, No. 7* (1919, cat. no. 20), *Series I, No. 8* (1919, cat. no. 21), and *Series I, No. 12* (1920, cat. no. 22).

In 1986 she owned forty-one of the fifty-seven abstractions on paper and canvas that had been exhibited in 1923, and over the years she had made only a handful of these works public, including *No. 21 – Special*, *No. 22 – Special*, and *Red & Orange Streak / Streak*. Forty-four works in the 1923 exhibition, however, depicted recognizable subject matter, largely rendered with a degree of precision that had first appeared in O'Keeffe's work in 1919, as in *Red Canna* (1919, fig. 18). Their subject matter was a marked contrast to her abstractions, and their relatively realistically rendered, tightly cropped forms may have derived from photographs and photographic techniques, with which she was becoming increasingly familiar.[55]

O'Keeffe's O'Keeffes

Figure 15
Petunias, 1925
Oil on board, 18 x 30
Fine Arts Museums of San Francisco,
Gift of the M. H. de Young Family
CR 491

As O'Keeffe became more and more aware of the way in which Stieglitz had interpreted her abstract work to certain critics – as a manifestation of her sexuality – she began producing paintings that in her mind could hardly be understood as anything but what they were – depictions of fruit and flowers.[56] But the critics overwhelmingly responded in Freudian terms to her representational as well as her abstract works in the 1923 exhibition. As a result, she limited the number of abstractions in subsequent exhibitions and in her work. And those she produced after 1924, such as *Red, Yellow and Black Streak* (1924, cat. no. 24), *Grey Blue & Black – Pink Circle* (1929, cat. no. 25), and *Winter Road I* (1963, cat. no. 73), do not consistently have the raw, expressive power of those she completed in the 1910s.[57] O'Keeffe never relinquished abstraction as a language of personal expression, but she shifted the emphasis in her work. After 1924 abstraction seldom functions as an expressive means in itself, but rather, it derives from the shapes of recognizable forms and becomes subordinate to their depiction, as in *Black Iris* (fig. 19).

That O'Keeffe retained more than two-thirds of the fifty-seven abstractions that were exhibited in 1923 is as important as the fact that she kept most of them out of the public eye for the next sixty years. Moreover, she

Figure 16
No. 9 Special, 1915
Charcoal on laid paper, 25 x 19 inches
The Menil Collection, Houston
CR 54

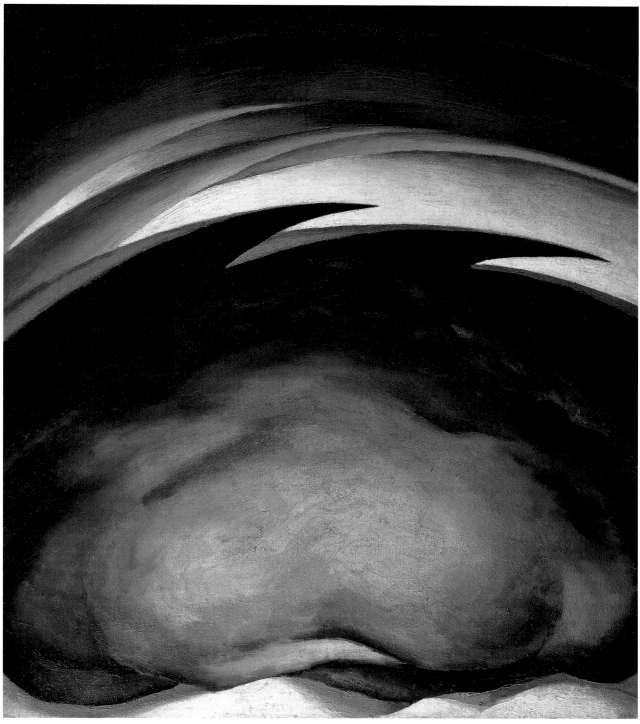

Figure 17
Series I – From the Plains, 1919
Oil on canvas, 27 x 23 inches
Private Foundation, extended loan,
Georgia O'Keeffe Museum, Santa Fe,
New Mexico
CR 288

Figure 18
Red Canna, 1919
Oil on canvas, 8 x 6 inches
Private collection, Las Vegas, extended loan,
Georgia O'Keeffe Museum, Santa Fe,
New Mexico, Courtesy Owings-Dewey
Fine Art, Santa Fe
CR 300

owned another thirty-three early abstractions that neither she nor Stieglitz ever exhibited, some of which are among her most outstanding achievements. These include *First Drawing of the Blue Lines* (1916, cat. no. 4), the pastels *Over Blue* (1918, fig. 20) and *Blue Flower* (1918, Juan and Anna Marie Hamilton, CR 259), as well as the series of watercolors she produced after moving to San Antonio, among which are *Untitled (Tree with Green Shade)* (1918, private foundation, CR 228), *Figures Under Rooftop* (1918, Georgia O'Keeffe Museum, CR 229), and *House with Tree – Red* (1918, cat. no. 10). These San Antonio works document an especially meaningful period in O'Keeffe's career because they mark her return to painting after four months of inactivity.[58]

O'Keeffe's secreting of these early abstractions and her decision to make them unavailable for exhibition are part of several strategies that she adopted soon after the 1923 exhibition in an attempt to discourage Freudian interpretations of her art. By keeping these works out of the public eye after 1923 and devoting most of her attention to the depiction of recognizable forms, she ultimately was successful in defining herself as a painter of landscapes, flowers, and bones.

However, O'Keeffe knew her early abstractions were important. As early as 1950 she gave The Metropolitan Museum of Art one of the charcoal abstractions of 1916/17 that she had produced while teaching in Texas, *No. 13 Special*. And in 1969, probably as a result of reacquainting herself with her early work in preparation for the Whitney show, she gave the Metropolitan another charcoal of 1916/17, *Abstraction*, as well as the remarkable watercolor *Blue Lines* (1916). That same year she gave an important early abstraction in oil to The Art Institute of Chicago, *Blue and Green Music* (1921). Finally, her bequests in 1979 included the abstractions *Red & Orange Streak / Streak* and the never-exhibited *Grey Line with Lavender and Yellow*.

In 1984 O'Keeffe wrote a codicil to her 1979 will that nullified her museum bequests, perhaps in response to the several overtures that had been made to her in the last years of her life to establish a museum in her name.[59] She may have hoped that such an institution would materialize before or shortly after she died, in which case all of the works in her collection could be kept together.[60] It is likely that O'Keeffe knew – as she had demonstrated in her broad-based selection of works for retrospectives, books, gifts, and bequests – that the less significant works in her collection were best understood when exhibited or reproduced within the

Figure 19
Black Iris, 1926
Oil on canvas, 36 x 29 ⅞ inches
The Metropolitan Museum of Art, New York,
Alfred Stieglitz Collection
CR 557

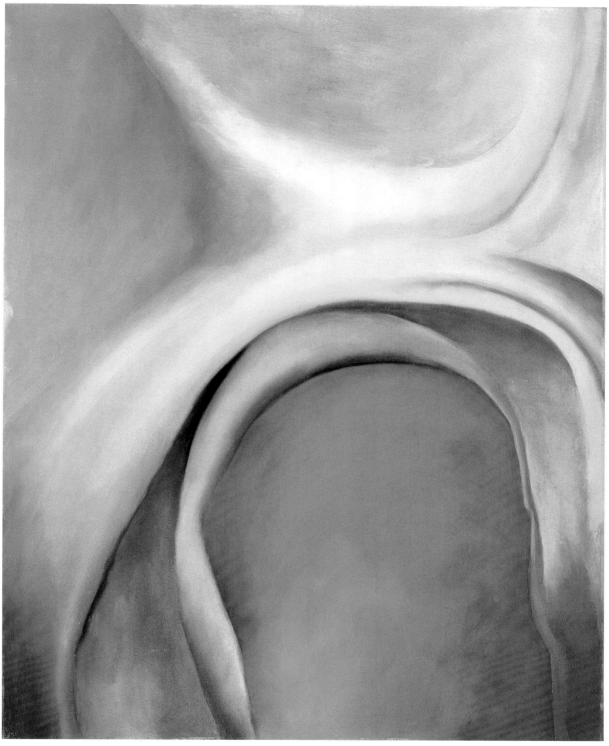

Figure 20
Over Blue, 1918
Pastel on paper, 27 ½ x 21 ½ inches
Private collection, Rochester, New York
CR 256

context of her finest achievements. An institution devoted to O'Keeffe did indeed come into being eleven years after her death; but by that time, many important works that O'Keeffe owned at the time of her death, and particularly many of her early abstractions, had already been distributed by her estate to a variety of national and international institutions (see Appendix V).

66 It may be that O'Keeffe intended the body of her collection to remain together, but what she specifically wished as its disposition will never be known. It is clear, however, that during the forty years she managed her career and made her living successfully through sales, she had carefully orchestrated and carried out a number of very specific strategies, some of which she had first learned from Stieglitz, that made it possible for her to sustain the financial security he had first established for her forty years before. At the same time, moreover, she also retained and kept out of the public eye a remarkable collection of works on paper and on canvas that accounted for a large component of her estate, which was valued in 1986 at approximately $70,000,000. The hundreds of works she kept included not only a broad range of her representational imagery, but also a remarkably large number of the works she had completed during the 1910s and early 1920s when she was most strongly committed to working in abstraction. Now that her formerly unknown works have become available, and especially those from the 1910s and early 1920s, it has become possible to redefine her achievement in ways that during her lifetime she took great pains to avoid.[61] As a result, O'Keeffe is increasingly recognized both as an artist whose work on paper was as important as her work in oil and as one of America's earliest and most important abstractionists. It is interesting to speculate what her career might have been had she not spent most of it publicly defining herself as an oil painter and a painter of recognizable forms.

Notes

1

All statistics in this essay regarding the nature and scope of O'Keeffe's collection of her work can be found in (or extracted from) information published in Barbara Buhler Lynes, *Georgia O'Keeffe: Catalogue Raisonné* (New Haven and London: Yale University Press, 1999).

2

Because of the onset of macular degeneration in the early 1970s, O'Keeffe was unable to work without assistance in oil after 1972.

3

Works selected for the exhibition come primarily from these two categories, but they also include two sculptures: *Abstraction* (1916, cat. no. 5) and *Abstraction* (1946, cat. no. 60).

4

See Barbara Buhler Lynes, "Inventions of Different Orders," and Judith C. Walsh, "The Language of O'Keeffe's Materials," in *O'Keeffe on Paper* (New York: Harry N. Abrams, 2000), pp. 39–56, 57–80.

5

For a discussion of Stieglitz's promotional efforts regarding O'Keeffe, see Barbara Buhler Lynes, *O'Keeffe, Stieglitz and the Critics: 1916–1929* (Ann Arbor: UMI Research Press, 1989; Chicago: University of Chicago Press, 1991).

6

For a discussion of O'Keeffe's and Irvine's efforts, see Lynes, "Preface," in *Catalogue Raisonné* (note 1), pp. 11–21.

7

Ibid., p. 13.

8

Ibid., Appendix III, pp. 1108–33.

9

Irvine's fact sheets have been available since 1946 at the Frances Mulhall Achilles Library, Whitney Museum of American Art, New York, but the full extent of O'Keeffe inscriptions on works (versos, backings, and stretchers) was not known until the publication of the catalogue raisonné in 1999. See ibid., pp. 11–21.

10

Ralph Flint, "Lily Lady Goes West," *Town and Country* 98 (January 1943), pp. 34, 64–65.

11

"Money Is Not Enough," *Time* 45 (February 5, 1945), p. 86.

12

The one-person exhibition that Stieglitz organized in 1917 generated the first sale of O'Keeffe's art, and within ten years, a strong market for it had developed. As O'Keeffe later pointed out: "I've made my living selling my paintings since 1927." Mary Lynn Kotz, "Georgia O'Keeffe at 90: 'Filling a Space in a Beautiful Way. That's What Art Means to Me,'" *Art News* 76 (December 1977), pp. 36–45. See also Lynes, *O'Keeffe, Stieglitz and the Critics* (note 5), p. 340, n. 23.

13

O'Keeffe received the Art Students League's William Merritt Chase Still-Life Prize for her painting *Untitled (Dead Rabbit with Copper Pot)* (1908, Art Students League, New York, CR 39). The abbreviation CR provides the reader with a reference to a reproduction of the image in the catalogue raisonné. CR is included after the date of a work named in this essay only if the work is not reproduced here or listed in the essay appendices.

14

O'Keeffe and Stieglitz began exchanging letters in January 1916 – and their correspondence continued when they were apart until his death in 1946.

15

In addition to her abstractions, O'Keeffe depicted animal and human figures, architecture, bones, feathers, flowers, fruit, landscapes, leaves, rocks, shells, and trees.

16

See Lynes, "Preface," in *Catalogue Raisonné* (note 1), pp. 13–14.

17

O'Keeffe annotated relevant fact sheets in her records to identify which works she destroyed. For information about them, see Lynes, "Appendix II," in ibid., pp. 1100–1107.

18

In an October 1955 letter to her sister, Claudia, O'Keeffe pointed out: "[I] went through all my paintings and destroyed many." The original letter is housed at the Georgia O'Keeffe Museum Research Center, Santa Fe, New Mexico.

19

O'Keeffe was keenly interested in the condition of her works and often had them cleaned or otherwise treated by conservators, including Felrath Hines, Sheldon and Caroline Keck, and Jean Volkmer.

20

The Downtown Gallery financial records are housed at The Archives of American Art, Washington, DC.

21

For O'Keeffe's comments about Stieglitz's reluctance to part with her work, see Perry Miller Adato (producer and director), *Georgia O'Keeffe,* videotape, 59 min., produced by WNET/THIRTEEN for Women in Art, 1977, Portrait of an Artist, no. 1, Series distributed by Films, Inc./Home Vision, New York.

22

Other oils that were priced at $8,000 are: *Red Poppy* (1928, Museum of Fine Arts, St. Petersburg, Florida, CR 638), *Dark Tree Trunks* (1946), *Black Patio Door* (1955, Amon Carter Museum, Fort Worth, Texas, CR 1283), *Blue – A* (1959), and *It Was Yellow and Pink II* (1959).

23

The others priced at $800 are: three watercolors measuring 11 7/8-by-8 7/8 inches, titled *Light Coming on the Plains (I–III)* (1917, Amon Carter Museum, Fort Worth, Texas, CR 209–11), and the 16-by-30-inch oil *Sand Hill, Alcalde* (1930, private collection, CR 726).

24

For exhibitions that took place during the period that Halpert was O'Keeffe's agent, see Lynes, *Catalogue Raisonné* (note 1), pp. 1153–56.

25

O'Keeffe was not an easy person to get along with, and thus, she often ended personal and/or professional relationships rather precipitously.

26

These include, for example, *Morning Sky with Houses, Lake George with Crows* (1921, cat. no. 37), *Autumn Trees – The Maple* (1924), *Black Lava Bridge, Hāna Coast – No. 2* (1939) *An Orchid,* and *Black Place III.*

27

Unpublished correspondence and other documents owned by The Georgia O'Keeffe Foundation, however, include records of specific works O'Keeffe loaned to her sister, Anita O'Keeffe Young, in which the works are ranked and assigned values.

28

O'Keeffe made works available to Bry that she had not made available to Irvine or Halpert, and Bry made entries for them in O'Keeffe's records. These entries refer to many but not all works on paper that O'Keeffe completed in the 1910s. Yet, in spite of forty years of record-keeping, O'Keeffe never documented more than fifty finished works she produced on canvas or paper.

29

For a discussion of the history of the records kept of O'Keeffe's works, see Lynes, "Preface," in *Catalogue Raisonné* (note 1), pp. 14–17.

30

The Whitney show was circulated to The Art Institute of Chicago and the San Francisco Museum of Art in 1971. Subsequent references to this exhibition are understood to include the New York, Chicago, and San Francisco venues.

31

In discussing the installation of the Whitney exhibition in New York with Nessa Forman, O'Keeffe pointed out: "The museum people started to hang the show chronologically. I didn't think it looked well. So I had it rearranged. I do it better than most people anyway." See Nessa Forman, "Georgia O'Keeffe and Her Art: 'Paint What's in Your Head,'" *Philadelphia Museum Bulletin,* October 22, 1971). And in an article Calvin Tomkins wrote in 1974, he quoted a museum director as having said: "Dealing with Georgia is very easy, provided you do exactly what she wants." See Calvin Tomkins, "The Rose in the Eye Looked Pretty Fine," *New Yorker* 50, 4 (March 1974), pp. 40–66. Bry played a major role in helping O'Keeffe organize the 1970 Whitney exhibition.

32

O'Keeffe often made the sale of at least one of her works a condition for her cooperation with an exhibition. In 1966, for example, the Fort Worth Art Museum agreed to purchase the watercolor series *Light Coming on the Plains (I–III)* and the oil painting *Black Patio Door.*

33

Later, *It Was Red and Pink* and *It Was Blue and Green* were given to, respectively, the Milwaukee Art Museum, and The Whitney Museum of American Art; *Evening Star No. V* was given to the McNay Art Museum, San Antonio, Texas; *Grey Lines with Black, Blue and Yellow* was given to the Museum of Fine Arts, Houston, and *Purple Hills* was given to the San Diego Museum of Art.

34

In fact, O'Keeffe kept specific work off the market in spite of receiving substantial offers for it.

35

Georgia O'Keeffe, *Some Memories of Drawings,* ed. Doris Bry (New York: Atlantis Editions, 1974; Albuquerque: The University of New Mexico Press, 1988); Georgia O'Keeffe, *Georgia O'Keeffe* (New York: The Viking Press, 1976). Earlier, in the 1960s, O'Keeffe selected twenty charcoal drawings for inclusion in two portfolios of ten works each; the first was published in 1968. Thereafter, all twenty drawings were reproduced in 1974 in *Some Memories of Drawings.*

36

Among the works that had not previously been acknowledged as such (some of which remained in her collection at her death) are: *No. 8 – Special* (1916, Whitney Museum of American Art, New York, CR 118), *No. 13 Special* (1916/17), *No. 14 Special* (1916), *Alligator Pear* (1922), *City Night, 2 Calla Lilies on Pink, Shell, No. I, Red and Yellow Cliffs Ghost Ranch* (1940), *Red Hills with the Pedernal* (1936), *Gerald's Tree I* (1937, Georgia O'Keeffe Museum, Santa Fe, New Mexico, CR 936), *Pelvis III* (1944, private collection, CR 1077), *Pedernal* (1945, cat. no. 68), *Dead Tree with Pink Hill* (1945), *In the Patio IX* (1950), *Drawing III* (1959), *Flag Pole and White House* (1959, Georgia O'Keeffe Museum, Santa Fe, New Mexico, CR 1369), *Winter Road I,* and *Black Rock with Blue Sky and White Clouds* (1972).

37

O'Keeffe, *Georgia O'Keeffe* (note 35), text accompanying plates 51 and 52; and text accompanying plate 59.

38

Artist Juan Hamilton, who became O'Keeffe's assistant and friend in 1973 and, later, her companion and associate, was instrumental in helping the artist carry out many art, exhibition, publication, and promotional projects. Hamilton introduced O'Keeffe to the medium of clay in the 1970s, with which O'Keeffe worked through 1984, and served as executor of her estate.

39
See, for example: Tomkins (note 31), pp. 40–66; Sanford Schwartz, "When New York Went to New Mexico," *Art in America* 64 (July/August 1976), pp. 93–97; Kotz (note 12), pp. 36–45; and Barbara Rose, "O'Keeffe's Trail," *New York Review of Books* 24 (March 31, 1977), pp. 29–33.

40
See Lynes, *O'Keeffe, Stieglitz and the Critics* (note 5).

41
Shortly after the publication of these books, however, O'Keeffe worked with The Metropolitan Museum of Art to organize a major exhibition of Stieglitz photographs. See New York, The Metropolitan Museum of Art, *Georgia O'Keeffe: A Portrait by Alfred Stieglitz* (New York, 1978), unpag.

42
See, for example: Judy Chicago and Miriam Schapiro, "Female Imagery," *Womanspace Journal* 1 (Summer 1973), pp. 11, 13; Judy Chicago, *Through the Flower: My Struggle as a Woman Artist* (Garden City, New York: Doubleday & Co., 1975); and Lucy Lippard, *From the Center: Feminist Essays on Women's Art* (New York: E. P. Dutton, 1976). And for an examination of O'Keeffe's relationship to feminism, see Barbara Buhler Lynes, "O'Keeffe and Feminism: A Problem of Position," in *The Expanding Discourse: Feminism and Art History,* eds. Norma Broude and Mary D. Garrard (New York: HarperCollins, 1992), pp. 436–49.

43
O'Keeffe to Barnes, June 22, 1947, Alfred Stieglitz/Georgia O'Keeffe Archive, Beinecke Rare Book and Manuscript Library, Yale University, New Haven, Connecticut.

44
See Lynes, *Catalogue Raisonné* (note 1), catalogue entries CR 57, 58. Macmahon, who taught political science at Columbia University, met O'Keeffe in 1914, when he was teaching at the University of Virginia. He taught there again in the summer of 1915 – when these pastels were made – and visited her during Thanksgiving that year, after she had moved to South Carolina to teach. O'Keeffe to Anita Pollitzer, October 1915, in *Lovingly Georgia: The Complete Correspondence of Georgia O'Keeffe & Anita Pollitzer,* ed. Clive Giboire, introduction by Benita Eisler (New York: Simon & Schuster, 1990), p. 48.

45
Although O'Keeffe had sold *Jack-in-Pulpit No. 1* (1930, cat. no. 43), it has been included here although it was not among the works O'Keeffe owned at the time of her death, first because she made several efforts to repurchase the work, and second, because including it indicates the progression in which these works in this series were painted – from realistic to abstract.

46
O'Keeffe, *Georgia O'Keeffe* (note 35), text accompanying plate 41.

47
Records on file at the Saint Louis Museum of Art, relating to the history of this work, verify O'Keeffe's attempts to reacquire it.

48
O'Keeffe, *Georgia O'Keeffe* (note 35), text accompanying plate 6.

49
O'Keeffe, *Some Memories of Drawings* (note 35), p. 102.

50
Of the hundreds of photographs that were made of her by various photographers over the years, only a few document O'Keeffe's sketching activity, such as those by photographers Ansel Adams and Todd Webb.

51
One occasion was in 1960, after O'Keeffe had just completed hundreds of new sketches and, in addition, had on file in her studio hundreds more from earlier periods. In response to a direct question as to whether she made preliminary drawings, she stated: "I make little drawings that have no meaning for anyone but me. They usually get lost when I don't need them any more. If you saw them, you'd wonder what those few little marks meant, but they do mean something to me." See Katherine Kuh, "Georgia O'Keeffe," in *The Artist's Voice: Talks with Seventeen Artists* (New York: Harper & Row, 1960), pp. 189–203. O'Keeffe also referred to sketches made during her first world travels in 1959 /60, while observing the earth from the window of an airplane: "I made many drawings about one and a half inches square of the rivers seen from the air." See O'Keeffe, *Georgia O'Keeffe* (note 35), text accompanying plate 103. See also New York, Hirschl & Adler Galleries, *Georgia O'Keeffe: Selected Works on Paper* (New York, 1986).

52
Because the contents of these folders no longer match their descriptive labels, O'Keeffe's original ordering has been lost.

53
This work had been no. 115 in "1946 Annual Exhibition of Contemporary American Painting," Whitney Museum of American Art, New York, December 10, 1946, January 16, 1947, and no. 23 in "An Exhibition of Painting & Sculpture Commemorating the Armory Show of 1913 and the First Exhibition of the Society of Independent Artists in 1917 with works by Members who Exhibited there," New York, American Academy of Arts and Letters, December 2, 1955.

54
Between 1915 and June 1918, O'Keeffe produced approximately twenty-four works in charcoal, two pastels, one hundred and eleven watercolors, and eight oils;

70

between June 1918 and 1972, O'Keeffe produced one hundred and thirty-eight oils, nine charcoals, eighteen pastels, and eighteen watercolors. See Lynes, "Inventions of Different Orders" (note 4), pp. 39–56.

55
For a study of the relationship of O'Keeffe's early work to photography, see Sarah Whitaker Peters, *Becoming O'Keeffe* (New York: Abbeville Press, 1991) and Elizabeth Hutton Turner, in *Georgia O'Keeffe & Alfred Stieglitz: Two Lives, A Conversation in Paintings and Photographs* (New York: HarperCollins/ Callaway Editions, in association with The Phillips Collection, 1992).

56
Stieglitz believed he had discovered America's first modernist woman artist in O'Keeffe, and he articulated his thinking about the nature of her accomplishment unequivocally for the first time in a 1919 essay entitled "Woman in Art," which equated O'Keeffe's art with her body. See Alfred Stieglitz, "Woman in Art" (unpublished essay, 1919), partially printed in Dorothy Norman, *Alfred Stieglitz: An American Seer* (New York: Random House, 1973), pp. 136–38. Two years later, in 1921, he provided visual equivalents for this idea when he exhibited his photographs at The Anderson Galleries in New York, including not only images of O'Keeffe's work, but also ones of her posed in front of her work in various stages of undress.

57
See Barbara Buhler Lynes, *Georgia O'Keeffe,* Rizzoli Art Series, ed. Norma Broude (New York: Rizzoli International Publications, 1993). Although *Winter Road I* reads as an abstraction, it derives from the shape of the curve in the highway that O'Keeffe could see from the window of her bedroom in her Abiquiu house.

58
O'Keeffe became ill in November 1917 and did not work again until after she moved to San Antonio in late February 1918.

59
In 1987, with the settlement of the contestation of O'Keeffe's will, the museum bequests were reestablished. But by 1984 O'Keeffe had sold some of the works she named as bequests in 1979, including one work intended for the Museum of Fine Arts, Boston: *D. H. Lawrence Pine Tree* (1929, Wadsworth Atheneum, Hartford, Connecticut, CR 687); two works intended for the National Gallery of Art, Washington, DC: *Black and White* (1930, Whitney Museum of American Art, New York, CR 700) and *Cow's Skull on Red* (1931/36, Curtis Galleries, New York, CR 799); three works intended for The Museum of Modern Art, New York: *Summer Days* (1936, Whitney Museum of American Art, New York, CR 880), *Black Door with Snow,* and *Ladder to the Moon* (1958, Emily Fisher Landau, New York, CR 1335); and three works intended for The Art Institute of Chicago: *Pelvis III, White Patio with Red Door* (1960, Curtis Galleries, New York, CR 1445) and *Sky Above Clouds IV* (1965, The Art Institute of Chicago, CR 1498). (However, *Sky Above Clouds IV* was partially given to that institution by O'Keeffe in 1983.) The estate did not attempt to substitute other works for those that had been sold, with the exception that The Museum of Modern Art received *From a Day with Juan II* (CR 1626, 1976/77), in addition to what remained in O'Keeffe's collection that had been specified for this institution. But ten additional works were given to the Museum of Fine Arts, Museum of New Mexico, Santa Fe; and the University Art Museum, The University of New Mexico, both of which had been mentioned in O'Keeffe's 1979 will without naming specific works as bequests.

60
The Georgia O'Keeffe Museum, Santa Fe, New Mexico, was founded in 1997 by philanthropists Anne and John Marion. A number of individuals had discussed the idea of founding a wing in a museum or a museum in O'Keeffe's name with the artist and her associates, including Joseph Hirshhorn, Crosby Kemper, Emily Fisher Landau, and Gerald Peters.

61
The extent and character of O'Keeffe's collection were not known until thirteen years after her death, when the catalogue raisonné was published.

I have but one desire as a painter – that is to paint what I see, as I see it, in my own way, without regard for the desires or taste of the professional dealer or the professional collector. I attribute what little success I have had to this fact. I wouldn't turn out stuff for order, and I couldn't. It would stifle any creative ability I possess.

– Georgia O'Keeffe

The Early Years

Between 1915 and 1918, when O'Keeffe was either teaching or taking art classes, she explored abstraction as a means of self-expression. Her keen interest in abstraction as an expressive device distinguishes her work from the representational art of most of her American contemporaries, and establishes O'Keeffe as among the most innovative American artists of the period.

Her experiments began in the fall of 1915, when she held a private exhibition of her work in her room and realized that most of it had been made to please others. Inspired to chart a new direction that would be hers alone, she limited herself to charcoal on white paper and began a series of highly abstract drawings, examples of which she mailed to a friend in New York. The friend took them to photographer Alfred Stieglitz, who at this time was also America's leading proponent of modern art. Shortly thereafter, in May 1916, Stieglitz included ten of O'Keeffe's drawings in a group show at his famous gallery, 291.

O'Keeffe continued producing charcoal abstractions, but gradually extended her experiments to the medium of watercolor; by the fall of 1916, she had returned to a full complement of color. During this period she became increasingly sophisticated with watercolor, using it less to describe than to capture and convey her enthusiasm for the vast expanses of the sky and landscape that she experienced in Texas, where she lived and taught from the fall of 1916 to early 1918. Increasingly, however, recognizable forms also become part of her vocabulary, and although the most representational works of these years read equally well as abstractions, this period marks the beginning of a trend toward investigating certain aspects of both abstraction and representation – a trend that would characterize the remainder of her career.

1 No. 32 – Special

1915
Pastel on paper
14 ½ x 20 inches
National Museum of American Art
Washington, DC
CR 57

2 No. 20 –
From Music – Special

1915
Charcoal on paper
13 ½ x 11 inches
National Gallery of Art
Washington, DC
(exhibited only at the Georgia
O'Keeffe Museum)
CR 53

3   Early Abstraction

1915
Charcoal on paper
23 ¾ x 18 ⅜ inches
Milwaukee Art Museum
CR 50

4 First Drawing of the
   Blue Lines

1916
Charcoal on paper
24 ¾ x 18 ⅞ inches
National Gallery of Art
Washington, DC
(exhibited only at the Milwaukee
Art Museum)
CR 62

5 Abstraction

1916 (cast 1979/80)
White-lacquered bronze
10 x 10 x 1 ½ inches
The Georgia O'Keeffe Foundation
Abiquiu, New Mexico
CR 75

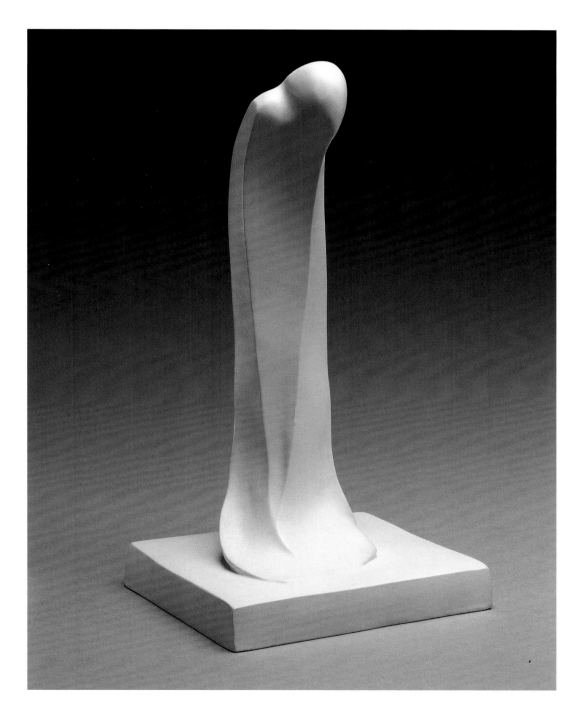

6 Sunrise and Little
Clouds No. II

1916
Watercolor on paper
8 7/8 x 12 inches
Georgia O'Keeffe Museum
Santa Fe
CR 134

7 Morning Sky
with Houses

1916
Watercolor and graphite on paper
8 7/8 x 12 inches
The Georgia O'Keeffe Foundation
Abiquiu, New Mexico
CR 127

8   Nude Series

1917
Watercolor on paper
12 x 8 ⅞ inches
Georgia O'Keeffe Museum
Santa Fe
CR 186

9   Evening Star No. VI   10   House with Tree – Red

1917   1918
Watercolor on paper   Watercolor on paper
8 7/8 x 12 inches   16 x 11 inches
Georgia O'Keeffe Museum   Museum of Fine Arts,
Santa Fe   Museum of New Mexico
CR 204   Santa Fe
                                   CR 233

Evening Star No. VI   House with Tree – Red

1917   1918
Watercolor on paper   Watercolor on paper
8 7/8 x 12 inches   16 x 11 inches
Georgia O'Keeffe Museum   Museum of Fine Arts,
Santa Fe   Museum of New Mexico
CR 204   Santa Fe
                                   CR 233

11 Untitled
    (Palo Duro Canyon)

    1916/17
    Graphite on paper
    3 ⅞ x 5 inches
    The Georgia O'Keeffe Foundation
    Abiquiu, New Mexico
    CR 144

12 Untitled
    (Palo Duro Canyon)

    1916/17
    Graphite on paper
    3 ⅞ x 5 inches
    The Georgia O'Keeffe Foundation
    Abiquiu, New Mexico
    CR 145

13 Untitled
(Palo Duro Canyon)

1916/17
Graphite on paper
3 ⅞ x 5 inches
The Georgia O'Keeffe Foundation
Abiquiu, New Mexico
CR 146

14 Untitled
(Palo Duro Canyon)

1916/17
Graphite on paper
3 ⅞ x 5 inches
The Georgia O'Keeffe Foundation
Abiquiu, New Mexico
CR 147

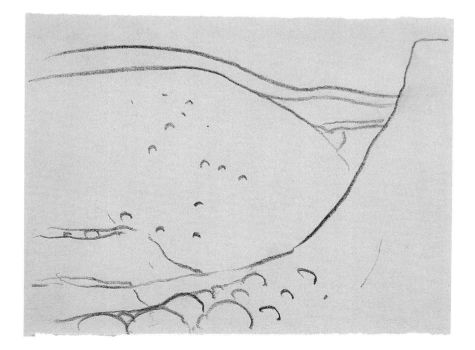

15 No. 20 – Special

1916/17
Oil on board
17 3/8 x 13 1/2 inches
Milwaukee Art Museum
CR 156

No. 21 – Special

1916/17
Oil on board
13 ½ x 16 ¼ inches
Museum of Fine Arts,
Museum of New Mexico
Santa Fe
CR 155

Painting is form, color,
pattern…. The subject
matter of a painting
should never obscure
its form and color,
which are its real
thematic contents,
since painting is a
different medium than
speech.

– Georgia O'Keeffe

New York

O'Keeffe moved to New York in June 1918 at the invitation of Alfred Stieglitz, and they were married in 1924. From mid-1918 until the summer of 1929, when O'Keeffe first traveled to New Mexico to paint, she and Stieglitz were nearly inseparable, living and working together either in the city (winter and spring) or at the Stieglitz family estate at Lake George (summer and fall).

Soon after her arrival in New York, O'Keeffe began working primarily in oil. Between 1918 and 1923, she produced in this medium some of the most remarkable abstractions of her entire career. But as early as 1919, a new degree of precision and specificity began to characterize her representational images, suggesting an active response to the concerns of Modernist photography.

In fact, as O'Keeffe became more and more aware of how her abstractions were being interpreted within the art community – as manifestations of female sexuality – she became increasingly committed to subject matter of recognizable forms, imagery that in her mind could hardly be understood as anything but what it was – for example, depictions of fruit and flowers. And after 1923, when the critics overwhelmingly responded in Freudian terms to both the representational and abstract works that Stieglitz included in her first large solo exhibition, she decided to limit her experimentations with abstraction and determined to make clear that the abstractions she subsequently made had objective sources. As a result, beginning in the mid-1920s, all but a handful of O'Keeffe's abstractions suggest their sources in the visible world and, thus, lack the raw, expressive power of her earlier ones.

This does not mean that O'Keeffe gave up abstraction as a language of personal expression, but that she shifted its emphasis in her work. After 1923, abstraction was seldom allowed to function as an expressive means in itself; rather, it derived from and became subordinate to the recognizable forms O'Keeffe chose to paint.

And so it was in the 1920s that O'Keeffe established herself principally as a painter of recognizable forms, for which she remains best known today. She developed approaches to representation during this decade that reveal her ongoing fascination with Modernist photography. Her large-scale paintings of flowers, leaves, and trees frequently present close-up views of these natural forms, and many of her paintings of New York buildings use optical distortions that are equally derivative of photographic manipulations.

17   Series I – No. 2

1918
Oil on board
20 x 16 inches
Milwaukee Art Museum
CR 262

18   Series I – No. 3

1918
Oil on board
20 x 16 inches
Milwaukee Art Museum
CR 254

19 Series 1, No. 4

1918
Oil on canvas
20 x 16 inches
Städtische Galerie im
Lenbachhaus
Munich
CR 255

20 Series I, No. 7

1919
Oil on board
20 x 16 inches
Milwaukee Art Museum
CR 279

Series 1, No. 4

Series I, No. 7

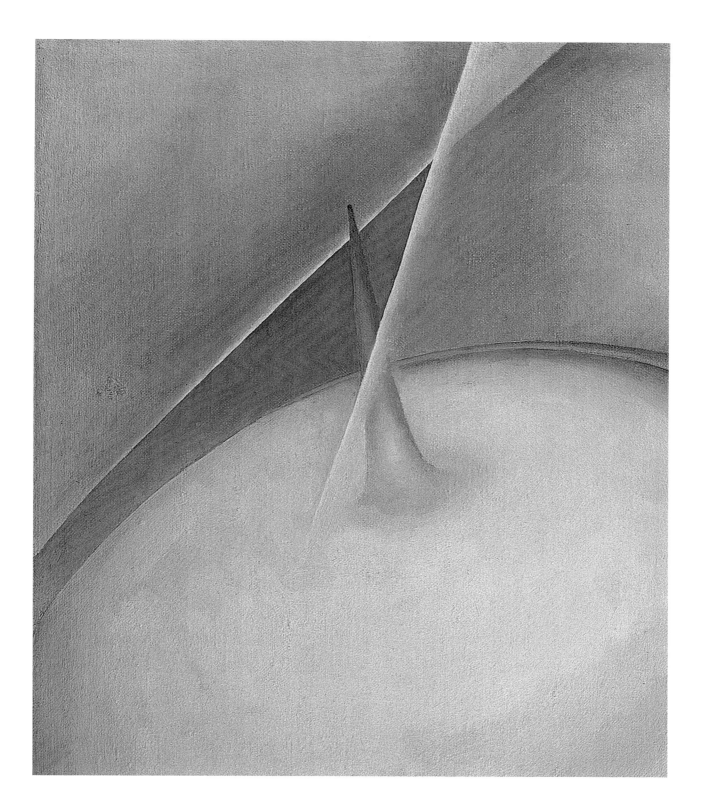

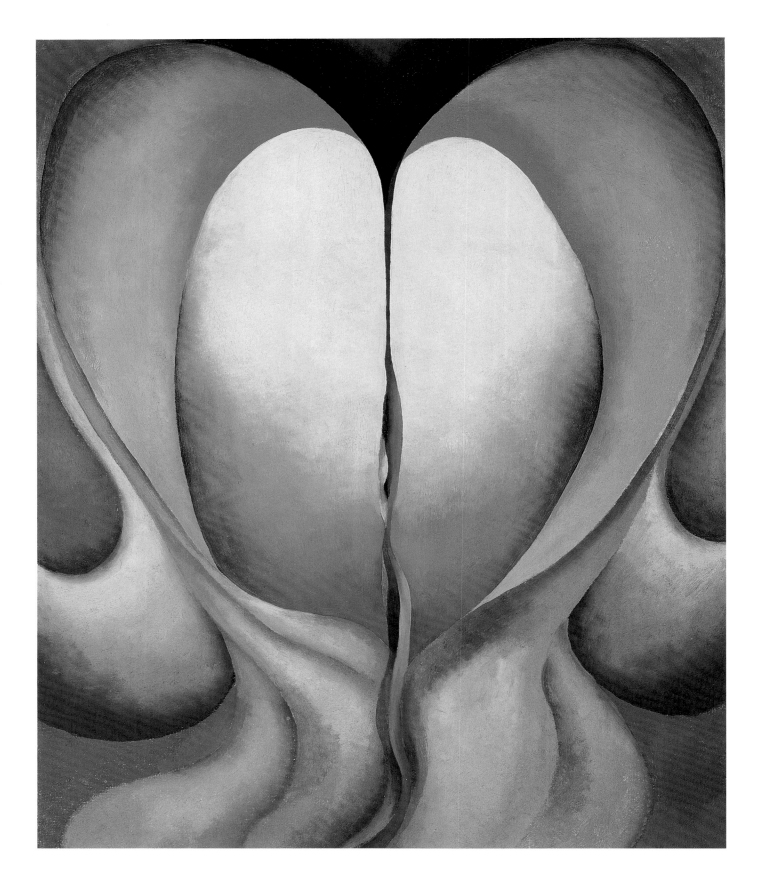

1919
Oil on canvas
20 x 16 inches
Städtische Galerie im
Lenbachhaus
Munich
CR 293

1920
Oil on canvas
20 x 16 ¼ inches
Georgia O'Keeffe Museum
Santa Fe
CR 311

23 **From the Lake, No. 3**

1924
Oil on canvas
36 x 30 inches
Philadelphia Museum of Art
CR 471

24 Red, Yellow and
Black Streak

1924
Oil on canvas
39 3/8 x 31 3/4 inches
Musée national d'art moderne,
Centre Georges Pompidou
Paris
CR 469

25 Grey Blue & Black –
Pink Circle

1929
Oil on canvas
36 x 48 inches
Dallas Museum of Art
CR 651

26　Apple Family – 2

1920
Oil on canvas
8 ⅛ x 10 ⅛ inches
Georgia O'Keeffe Museum
Santa Fe
CR 315

27　Apple Family 3

1921
Oil on canvas
7 ⅞ x 10 ⅞ inches
Milwaukee Art Museum
CR 347

28 Tan Clam Shell
with Seaweed

1926
Oil on canvas
9 x 7 inches
The Georgia O'Keeffe Foundation
Abiquiu, New Mexico
CR 535

29 Clam Shell

1930
Oil on canvas
24 x 36 inches
The Metropolitan Museum of Art
New York
CR 707

30 Seaweed

1927
Oil on canvas
9 x 7 inches
Iris & B. Gerald Cantor Center for
Visual Arts at Stanford University
Palo Alto, California
CR 604

31 Canna Leaves

1925
Oil on canvas
26 x 11 inches
Georgia O'Keeffe Museum
Santa Fe
CR 503

1928
Oil on canvas
40 x 30 ⅛ inches
Brooklyn Museum of Art
New York
CR 640

1931
Oil on canvas
20 x 17 inches
Museum of Fine Arts,
Museum of New Mexico
Santa Fe
CR 787

34   Grey and Brown Leaves

1929
Oil on canvas
36 x 30 inches
Milwaukee Art Museum
CR 676

35 Birch and Pine Tree, No. 2

1925
Oil on canvas
36 x 22 inches
The Rahr-West Art Museum
Manitowoc, Wisconsin
CR 508

36 Last Yellow White Birch

1928
Oil on canvas
36 x 29 ¾ inches
Private collection
CR 645

37 Lake George with
Crows

1921
Oil on canvas
28 ½ x 25 inches
National Gallery of Canada
Ottawa
(exhibited only at the
Georgia O'Keeffe Museum)
CR 358

38 Corn, No. 2

1924
Oil on canvas
27 ¼ x 10 inches
Georgia O'Keeffe Museum
Santa Fe
CR 454

39 Lake George Autumn

1927
Oil on canvas
17 x 32 inches
Milwaukee Art Museum
CR 607

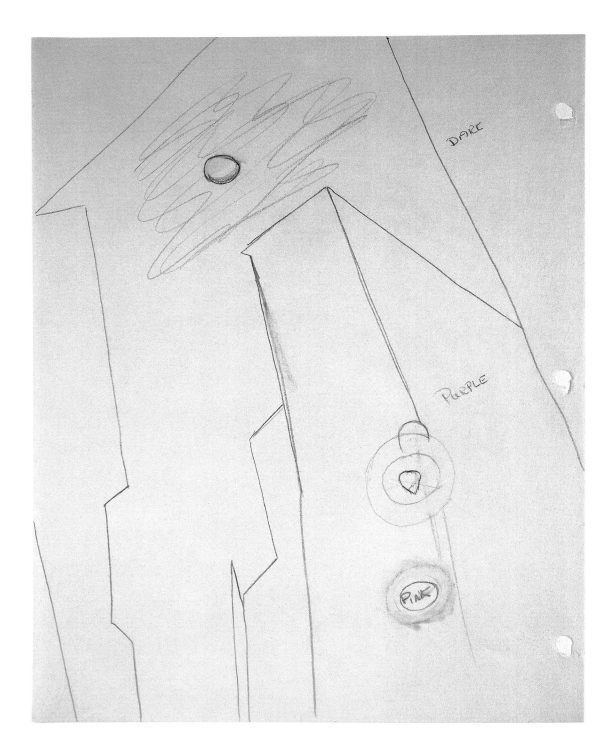

40 Untitled (New York
Street with Moon)

1925
Graphite on paper
11 x 8 ½ inches
The Georgia O'Keeffe Foundation
Abiquiu, New Mexico
CR 482

41 River, New York

1928
Oil on canvas
12 x 32 inches
The Metropolitan Museum of Art
New York
CR 619

42 Abstraction White Rose

1927
Oil on canvas
36 x 30 inches
Georgia O'Keeffe Museum
Santa Fe
CR 599

45 Jack-in-the-Pulpit
    No. VI

1930
Oil on canvas
36 x 18 inches
National Gallery of Art
Washington, DC
CR 720

46 White Pansy

1927
Oil on canvas
36 x 30 inches
The Cleveland Museum of Art
CR 590

47 2 Calla Lillies on Pink

1928
Oil on canvas
40 x 30 inches
Philadelphia Museum of Art
CR 629

A Sunflower from
Maggie

1937
Oil on canvas
15 x 20 inches
Museum of Fine Arts
Boston
CR 922

It takes courage to be
a painter. I always felt
I walked on the edge
of a knife.

– Georgia O'Keeffe

New
Mexico

In 1917, when O'Keeffe traveled from Texas to vacation in Colorado, she spent several days in New Mexico, for which she felt an immediate affinity. She returned twelve years later, in 1929, to spend the first of many summers painting there. In 1949, three years after Stieglitz's death, she made New Mexico her permanent home.

In 1929 O'Keeffe bought a car and learned to drive, but worked primarily in and around Taos, making paintings of various architectural, tree, and landscape forms that interested her. By the early 1930s, she had begun to explore areas south of Taos, such as Alcalde, Española, and Santa Fe. In the mid-1930s, she discovered regions to the south and west of Taos that were clearly her favorites and served as inspiration for her work over the next forty years. She was particularly drawn to the stark, but richly colored red and yellow hills and cliffs of the Ghost Ranch area and its flat-topped mountain, Cerro Pedernal; the white jagged cliff formations near the village of Abiquiu; the black hills of the Navajo country, some 150 miles west of Ghost Ranch; the cedar trees surrounding the Ghost Ranch house; and the bleached desert bones she collected as she roamed the desert. All became frequent subjects in her work through the 1940s.

O'Keeffe purchased a house at Ghost Ranch in 1940, and one in the village of Abiquiu in 1945. After 1949 she lived summer and fall at Ghost Ranch and winter and spring in Abiquiu. From the early 1940s through the early 1960s, she often chose as the subject of her work the simple architectural forms of these houses as well as their surrounding landscape configurations and the cottonwood trees of the Chama River valley.

O'Keeffe began the first of several trips around the world in 1959, and the experience of seeing the earth and sky from the window of an airplane inspired a new and last series of paintings in the 1950s and 1960s. The landscape configurations recorded in these works are highly simplified and easily read as pure abstractions, suggesting that her early interest in expression through essentially nonrepresentational means remained an important part of her thinking throughout her career.

49 Ranchos Church

1929
Graphite on paper
8 ½ x 10 inches
The Georgia O'Keeffe Foundation
Abiquiu, New Mexico
CR 661

50 Ranchos Church

1930
Oil on canvas
24 x 36 inches
The Metropolitan Museum of Art
New York
CR 704

51 **In the Patio VIII**

1950
Oil on canvas
26 x 20 inches
Georgia O'Keeffe Museum
Santa Fe
CR 1211

52 Patio Door with
    Green Leaf

53 Black Door with Snow

1956
Oil on canvas
36 x 30 inches
Georgia O'Keeffe Museum
Santa Fe
CR 1292

1955
Oil on canvas
36 x 30 inches
Eugene and Clare Thaw
Santa Fe
CR 1279

54 Horse's Skull with
    Pink Rose

    1931
    Graphite on paper
    10 x 8 ½ inches
    The Georgia O'Keeffe Foundation
    Abiquiu, New Mexico
    CR 774

55 Horse's Skull with
    Pink Rose

    1931
    Oil on canvas
    40 x 30 inches
    Los Angeles County Museum of Art
    CR 775

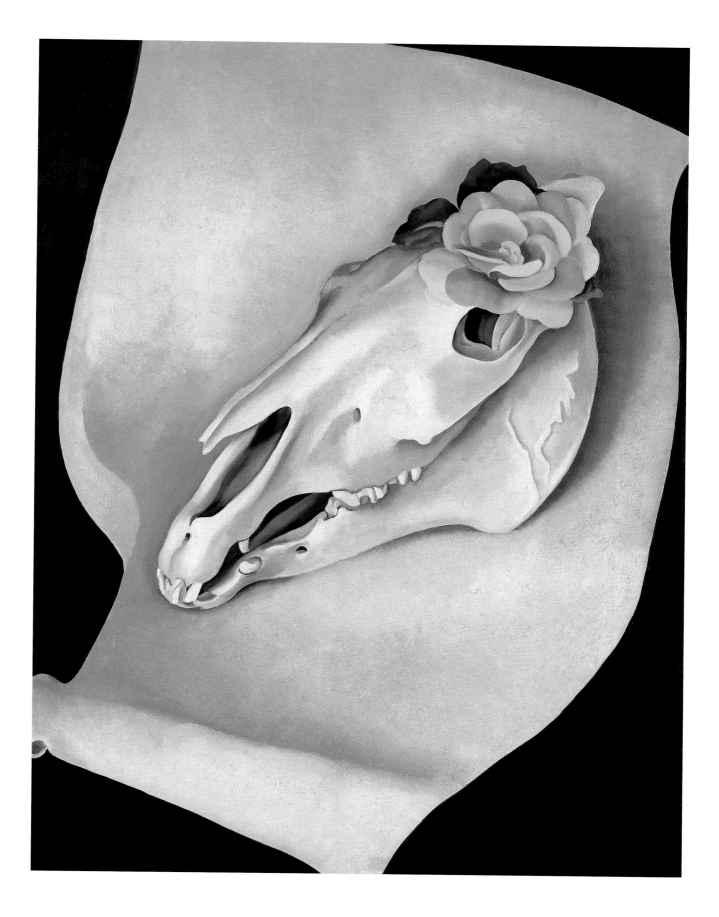

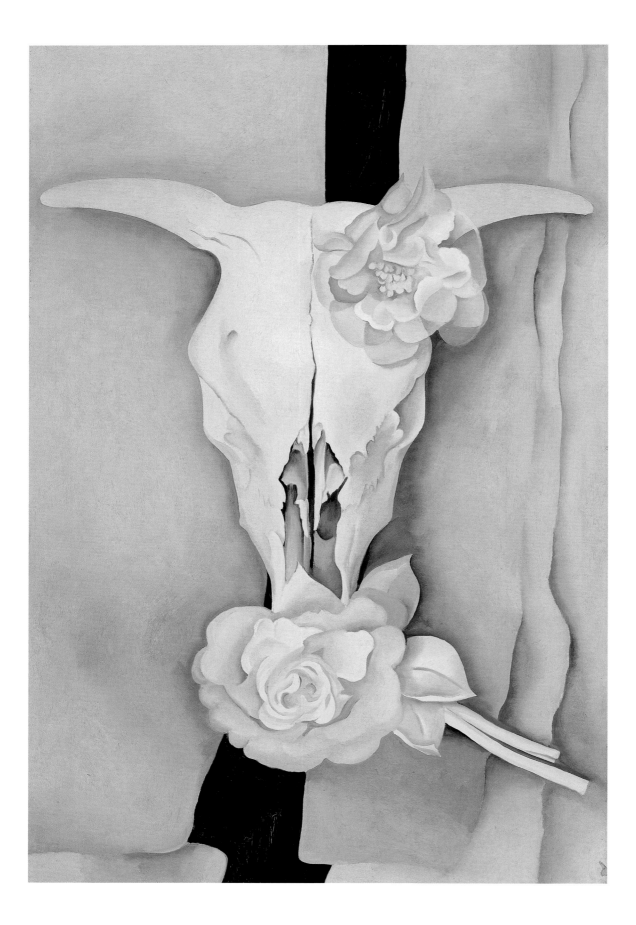

56 Cow's Skull with
Calico Roses

1931
Oil on canvas
36 x 24 inches
The Art Institute of Chicago
CR 772

57 Turkey Feathers in
Indian Pot

1935
Oil on canvas
24 x 8 ½ inches
Private collection
CR 855

58 Horizontal Horse's
or Mule's Skull
with Feather

1936
Oil on canvas
16 x 30 inches
Milwaukee Art Museum
CR 878

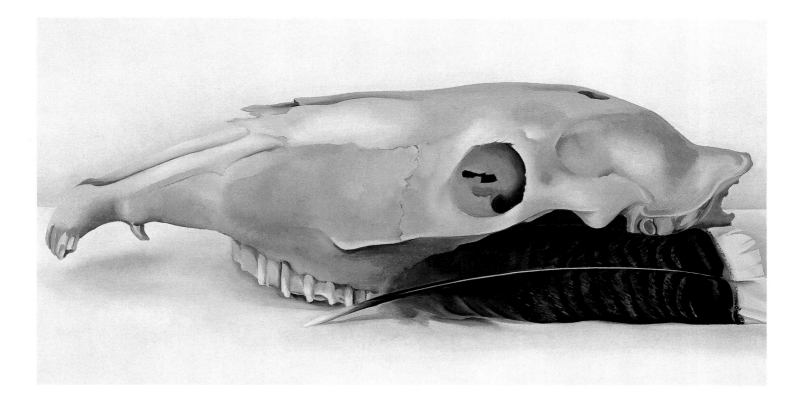

59 Pelvis IV

1944
Oil on masonite
36 x 40 inches
Georgia O'Keeffe Museum
Santa Fe
CR 1078

60 Abstraction

1946 (cast 1979/80)
White-lacquered bronze
36 x 36 x 4 ½ inches
The Georgia O'Keeffe Foundation
Abiquiu, New Mexico
CR 1135

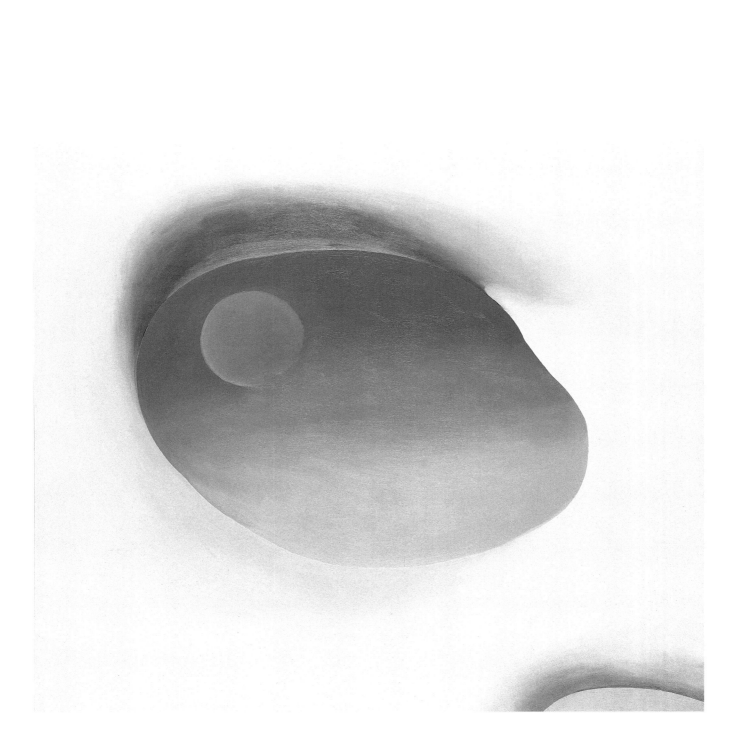

61 Small Purple Hills

1934
Oil on board
16 x 19 ¾ inches
Private collection
CR 838

62 Grey Wash Forms

1936
Oil on canvas
16 x 30 inches
Museum of Fine Arts
Boston
CR 897

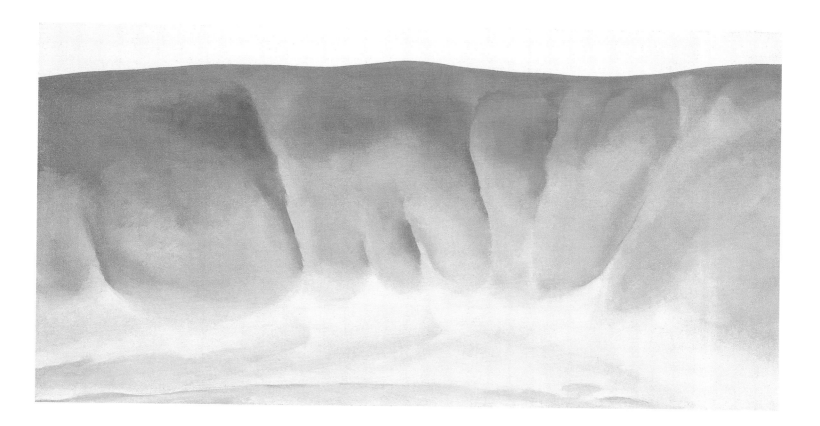

63 The Cliff Chimneys

1938
Oil on canvas
36 x 30 inches
Milwaukee Art Museum
CR 955

64 Untitled
(Red and Yellow Cliffs)

1940
Oil on canvas
24 x 36 inches
Georgia O'Keeffe Museum
Santa Fe
CR 998

1940
Oil on canvas
24 x 36 inches
Georgia O'Keeffe Museum
Santa Fe
CR 998

65 Untitled (Dry Waterfall, 66 Cliffs Beyond Abiquiu –
   Ghost Ranch)   Dry Waterfall

c. 1943   1943
Graphite and charcoal on paper   Oil on canvas
23 ⅞ x 17 ⅞ inches   30 x 16 inches
Georgia O'Keeffe Museum   The Cleveland Museum of Art
Santa Fe   CR 1061
CR 1071

Black Place III

1944
Oil on canvas
36 x 40 inches
Private Foundation, extended loan,
Georgia O'Keeffe Museum
Santa Fe
CR 1082

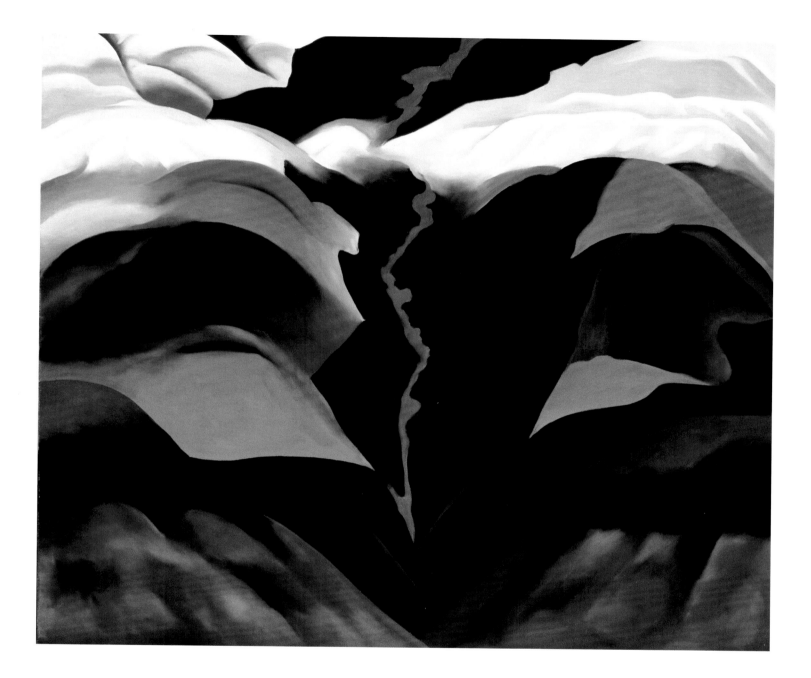

68 Pedernal

1945
Pastel on paper
21 ½ x 43 ¼ inches
Georgia O'Keeffe Museum
Santa Fe
CR 1117

69 Another Drawing
Similar Shape

1959
Charcoal on paper
24 ⅞ x 18 ⅝ inches
Milwaukee Art Museum
CR 1341

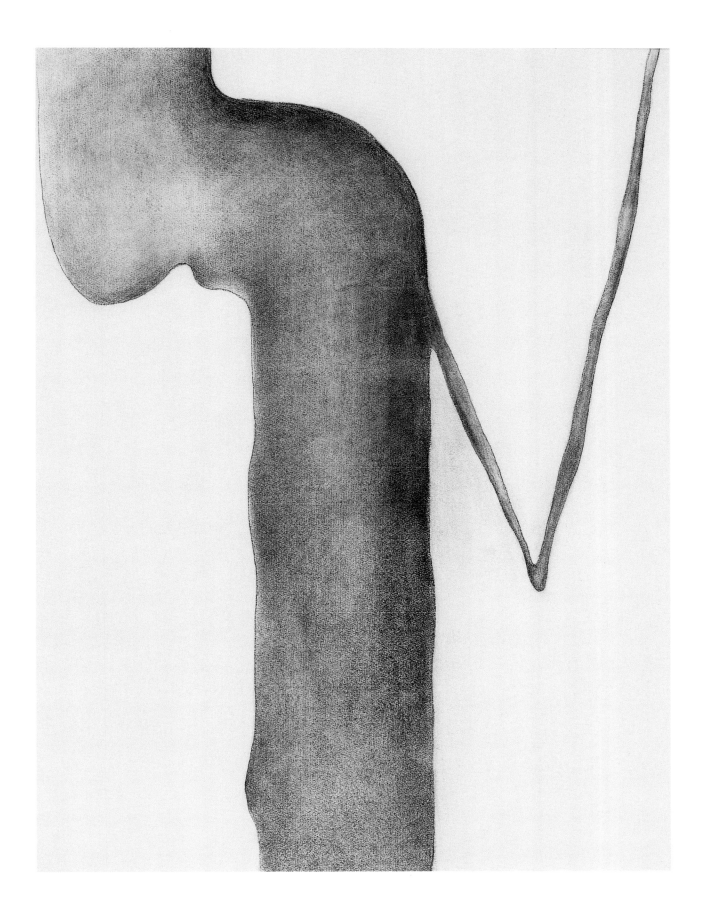

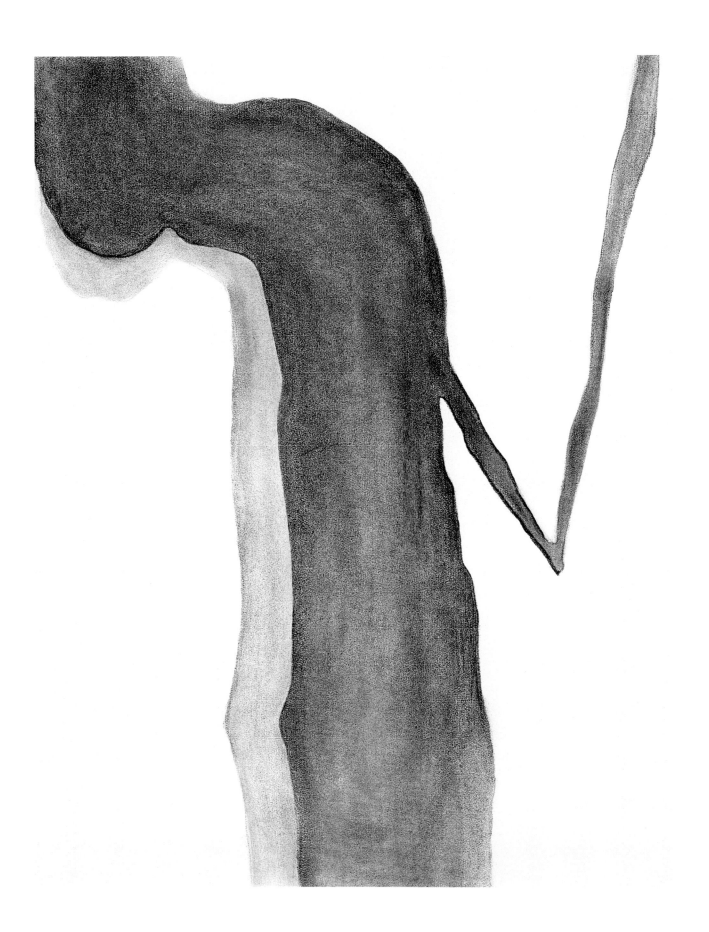

70 Drawing V

71 It Was Yellow and
    Pink III

1959
Charcoal on paper
24 ½ x 18 ¾ inches
Georgia O'Keeffe Museum
Santa Fe
CR 1339

1960
Oil on canvas
40 x 30 inches
The Art Institute of Chicago
CR 1442

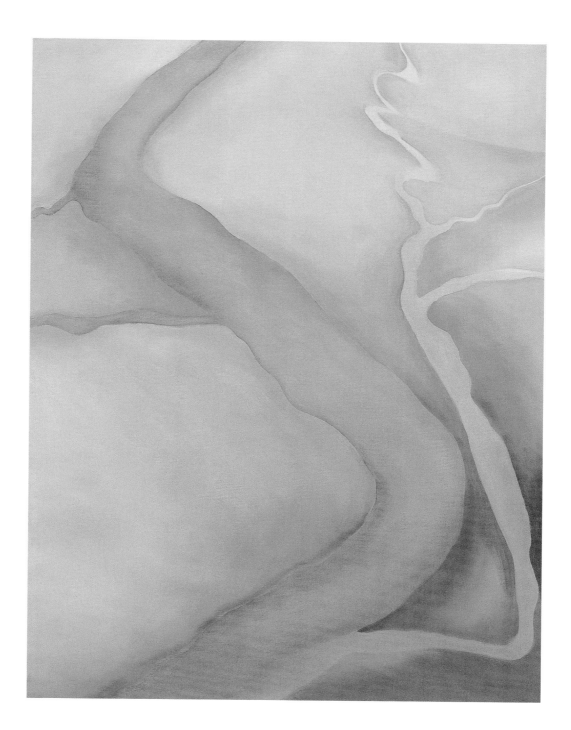

72 **Sky with Flat White Cloud**

1962
Oil on canvas
60 x 80 inches
National Gallery of Art
Washington, DC
CR 1473

73 **Winter Road I**

1963
Oil on canvas
22 x 18 inches
National Gallery of Art
Washington, DC
CR 1477

Appendices

Appendix I

Works Exhibited in the 1960, 1966, and 1970 Retrospectives

Works are listed by title, date, and in the order of their inclusion on exhibition checklists (the 1966 checklist was never numbered). Corresponding catalogue raisonné entry numbers are included in parentheses, followed by current catalogue raisonné title and/or date, if different from checklist entry.

1960 Worcester Art Museum, Worcester, Massachusetts, "Georgia O'Keeffe: Forty Years of Her Art"

1
Red and Orange Streak, 1919 (CR 287, Red & Orange Streak / Streak)

2
59th Street Studio, 1919 (CR 295, 59th St. Studio)

3
Lightning at Sea, 1922 (CR 386)

4
From the Lake No. III, 1924 (CR 471, From the Lake, No. 3)

5
New York Street with Moon, 1925 (CR 483)

6
Shell and Old Shingle No. I, 1926 (CR 540, Shell and Old Shingle I / Shell and Old Shingle No. I)

7
Shell and Old Shingle No. II, 1926 (CR 541, Shell & Old Shingle II / Shell and Old Shingle No. II)

8
Shell and Old Shingle No. III, 1926 (CR 542, Shell & Old Shingle III / Shell and Old Shingle No.3)

9
Shell and Old Shingle No. IV, 1926 (CR 543, Shell and Old Shingle IV / Shell and Old Shingle No. 4)

10
Shell and Old Shingle No. VII, 1926 (CR 546, Shell & Shingle Series VII)

11
Abstraction, White Rose, 1927 (CR 601, Ballet Skirt or Electric Light)

12
Seaweed, 1927 (CR 604)

13
Ranchos Church. Front, 1929 (CR 703, Ranchos Church, Front, 1930)

14
Black Cross with Red Sky, 1929 (CR 669, Cross with Red Sky)

15
Dark Mesa and Pink Sky, 1930 (CR 739, Dark Mesa with Pink Sky)

16
Purple Hills Near Abiquiu, 1935 (CR 870, Purple Hills)

17
Deer's Skull with Pedernal, 1936 (CR 879)

18
Summer Days, 1936 (CR 880)

19
Red Hills with White Cloud, 1937 (CR 930))

20
Pelvis with Shadows and the Moon, 1943 (CR 1052)

21
Cliffs Beyond Abiquiu, Dry Waterfall, 1943 (CR 1061, Cliffs Beyond Abiquiu – Dry Waterfall)

22
Dead Cottonwood Tree, 1943 (CR 1065)

23
My Heart, 1944 (CR 1074)

24
Pelvis IV, 1944 (CR 1078)

25
Black Place III, 1944 (CR 1082)

26
Pelvis Series, Red with Yellow, 1945 (CR 1106)

27
Red Hills and Sky, 1945 (CR 1114)

28
A Black Bird with Snow-Covered Red Hills, 1946 (CR 1148)

29
In the Patio I, 1946 (CR 1146)

30
Black Place Green, 1949 (CR 1175)

31
Poppies, 1950 (CR 1214)

32
Wall with Green Door, 1952 (CR 1265)

33
Antelope, 1954 (CR 1273)

34
Winter Cottonwoods East, V, 1954 (CR 1276, Winter Cottonwoods East V)

35
Black Patio Door, 1955 (CR 1283)

36
It Was Red and Pink, 1959 (CR 1358)

37
It Was Yellow and Pink, 1960 (CR 1442, It Was Yellow and Pink III)

38
It Was Blue and Green, 1960 (CR 1444)

39
White Patio with Red Door, 1960 (CR 1445)

40
Ram's Horns, 1949 (?) (either CR 1176, Ram's Horns I, c. 1949 or CR 1177, Ram's Horns II, c. 1949)

41
Antelope Horns, 1954 (CR 1252, c. 1952)

42
Drawing IX, 1959 (CR 1348)

43
Drawing X, 1959 (CR 1340)

1966 Amon Carter Museum of Western Art, Fort Worth, Texas, "Georgia O'Keeffe: An Exhibition of the Work of the Artist from 1915 to 1966"

Drawing No. 13, 1915 (CR 157, No. 13 Special, 1916/17)

Special No. 15, 1915 (CR 154, No. 15 Special, 1916/17)

Train at Night in the Desert, 1916 (CR 128)

Abstraction IX, 1916 (CR 99, Abstraction)

Blue Lines No. 10, 1916 (CR 64, Blue Lines)

Light Coming on the Plains No. I, 1917 (CR 209)

Light Coming on the Plains No. II, 1917 (CR 210, No. II Light Coming on the Plains)

Light Coming on the Plains No. III, 1917 (CR 211, No. III Light Coming on the Plains)

Roof with Snow, 1917 (CR 126, 1916)

Evening Star No. V, 1917 (CR 203)

Starlight Night, 1917 (CR 207)

Nude Series III, 1917 (CR 187, Nude No. III)

Nude Series VII, 1917 (CR 181)

Nude Series VIII, 1917 (CR 182, Nude Series, VIII)

Nude Series X, 1917 (CR 185)

Nude Series XI, 1917 (CR 179, Seated Nude, XI)

Nude Series XII, 1918 (CR 188, 1917)

59th Street Studio, 1919 (CR 295, 59th St. Studio)

Series I, No. 12, 1920 (CR 311)

Three Zinnias, 1920 (CR 353, 3 Zinnias, 1921)

Lake George with Crows, 1921 (CR 358)

Two Avocados, 1923 (CR 417, Alligator Pears)

From the Lake No. 3, 1924 (CR 471, From the Lake, No. 3)

Dark Abstraction, 1924 (CR 451)

Portrait of a Day, 3rd Day, 1924 (CR 450, Portrait of a Day – 3rd Day)

Birch and Pine Tree No. I, 1925 (CR 507, Birch and Pine Tree No. 1)

Grey Tree, Lake George, 1926 (CR 512, 1925)

Black Iris, 1926 (CR 557)

Shell and Old Shingle II, 1926 (CR 541, Shell & Old Shingle II / Shell and Old Shingle No. II)

Shell and Old Shingle III, 1926 (CR 542, Shell & Old Shingle III / Shell and Old Shingle No. 3)

Shelton with Sun Spots, 1926 (CR 527, The Shelton with Sun Spots, N.Y.)

East River from the Shelton (30th Story), 1926 (CR Appendix II, no. 83)

Closed Clam Shell, 1926 (CR 539)

Open Clam Shell, 1926 (CR 538)

Morning Glory with Black, c. 1926 (CR 561, White Flower)

Red Hills and the Sun, 1927 (CR 608, The Red Hills with Sun)

Seaweed, 1927 (CR 604)

Line and Curve, 1927 (CR 572)

White Birch, 1927 (CR 511, 1925)

Red Poppy, 1927 (CR 594)

Black Abstraction, 1927 (CR 574)

White Rose II, 1927 (CR 599, Abstraction White Rose)

White Rose III, 1927 (CR 601, Ballet Skirt or Electric Light)

Brown and Tan Leaves, 1928 (CR 641)

Single Lily with Red, 1928 (CR 633)

Lake George Window, 1929 (CR 653, Farmhouse Window and Door)

Black Cross, New Mexico, 1929 (CR 667, Black Cross)

Black Hollyhocks and Blue Larkspur, 1929 (CR 714, Black Hollyhock Blue Larkspur, 1930)

Abstraction, 1929 (CR 648)

Yellow Cactus Flower, 1929 (CR 675, Yellow Cactus)

Black and White, 1930 (CR 700)

Ranchos Church, Taos, 1930 (CR 704, Ranchos Church)

Clam Shell, 1930 (CR 707)

Dark Mesa and Pink Sky, 1930 (CR 739, Dark Mesa with Pink Sky)

Cow's Skull with Red, 1931/36 (CR 799, Cow's Skull on Red)

Cross by the Sea, Canada, 1931 (CR 813, 1932)

Green Mountains, Canada, 1932 (CR 818)

The White Trumpet Flower, 1932 (CR 816, The White Flower)

White Barn No. I, Canada, 1932 (CR 805, White Barn)

Barn with Snow, 1933 (CR 822, 1934)

Eagle Claw and Bean Necklace, 1934 (CR 829)

Special No. 40, 1935 (CR 821, 1934)

Rib and Jawbone, 1935 (CR 853)

Grey Hills II, 1936 (CR 897, Grey Wash Forms)

Mule's Skull with Turkey Feather, 1936 (CR 877, Mule's Skull with Turkey Feathers)

Red Hills with White Cloud, 1937 (CR 930)

Deer's Horn, Near Cameron, 1938 (CR 914, From the Faraway Nearby [Deer's Horns, Near Cameron], 1937)

Dead Cottonwood Tree, 1943 (CR 1065)

Cliffs Beyond Abiquiu – Dry Waterfall, 1943 (CR 1061)

Cliffs Beyond Abiquiu, 1943 (CR 1060)

The Black Place, 1943 (CR 1058)

Pelvis with the Moon, 1943 (CR 1050, Pelvis with the Moon – New Mexico)

Pelvis IV (Oval with Moon), 1944 (CR 1078, Pelvis IV)

Untitled 3, 1944 (CR 1074, My Heart)

Black Place III, 1944 (CR 1082)

Spring Tree No. II, 1945 (CR 1121)

Red Hills and Sky, 1945
(CR 1114)

Bare Tree Trunks with Snow, 1946
(CR 1151)

Spring, 1948 (CR 1163)

Winter Trees, Abiquiu I, 1950
(CR 1218, Winter Trees, Abiquiu, I)

Mesa and Road to the East II,
1952 (CR 1235, Mesa and Road
East II)

From the Plains No. I, 1953 (CR
1262, From the Plains, 1952/54)

Winter Cottonwoods Soft, 1954
(CR 1277, Winter Cottonwood
Trees Soft)

Antelope, 1954 (CR 1273)

Antelope Horns, 1954 (CR 1252,
c. 1952)

Winter Cottonwoods East, V, 1954
(CR 1276, Winter Cottonwoods
East V)

Green Patio Door, 1955
(CR 1282)

Black Patio Door, 1955
(CR 1283)

Pelvis Series, Red with Yellow,
1945 (CR 1106)

It Was Red and Pink, 1959
(CR 1358)

It Was Yellow and Pink III, 1960
(CR 1442)

White Patio with Red Door, 1960
(CR 1445)

Above the Clouds III, 1963
(CR 1479, Sky Above Clouds III /
Above the Clouds III)

The Winter Road, 1963
(CR 1477, Winter Road I)

Canyon Country, 1964 (CR 1504,
c. 1965)

Above the Clouds IV, 1966
(CR 1498, Sky Above Clouds IV,
1965)

**1970 Whitney Museum of
American Art, New York,
"Georgia O'Keeffe"**

1
Blue Lines, 1916 (CR 64)

2
Drawing No. 9, 1915 (CR 54,
No. 9 Special)

3
Drawing No. 13, 1915 (CR 157,
No. 13 Special, 1916/17)

4
Drawing No. 8, 1916 (CR 118,
No. 8 – Special)

5
Drawing No. 15, 1916 (CR 154,
No. 15 Special, 1916/17)

6
Blue No. I, 1916 (CR 91)

7
Blue No. II, 1916 (CR 92)

8
Blue No. III, 1916 (CR 93)

9
Blue No. IV, 1916 (CR 94)

10
Morning Sky with Houses and
Windmill, 1916 (CR Appendix II,
no. 3)

11
Painting No. 21, 1916 (CR 155,
No. 21 – Special, 1916/17)

12
Painting No. 22, 1916 (CR 160,
No. 22 – Special, 1916/17)

13
Drawing No. 12, 1917 (CR 117,
No. 12 Special, 1916)

14
Canyon with Crows, 1917
(CR 197)

15
Evening Star No. IV, 1917
(CR 202)

16
Evening Star No. V, 1917
(CR 203)

17
Evening Star No. VI, 1917
(CR 204)

18
Light Coming on the Plains No. II,
1917 (CR 210, No. II Light
Coming on the Plains)

19
Nude Series, VII, 1917 (CR 181,
Nude Series VII)

20
Starlight Night, 1917 (CR 207)

21
Orange and Red Streak, 1919
(CR 287, Red & Orange Streak /
Streak)

22
Black Spot No. 3, 1919 (CR 285)

23
Blue and Green Music, 1919
(CR 344, 1921)

24
Music – Pink and Blue No. I,
1919 (CR 257, 1918)

25
59th Street Studio, 1919
(CR 295, 59th St. Studio)

26
Series I, No. 12, 1920 (CR 311)

27
Lake George with Crows, c. 1921
(CR 358, 1921)

28
Abstraction of Stream, 1921
(CR 342)

29
Leaves Under Water, 1922
(CR 379)

30
Spring, c. 1922 (CR 401)

31
Grey Line with Black, Blue and
Yellow, c. 1923 (CR 447, Grey
Lines with Black, Blue and
Yellow, 1923/25)

32
Dark Abstraction, 1924 (CR 451)

33
Flower Abstraction, 1924
(CR 458)

34
From the Lake No. 3, 1924
(CR 471, From the Lake, No. 3)

35
Portrait of a Day – Third Day,
1924 (CR 450, Portrait of a Day –
3rd Day)

36
Red Yellow and Black Streak,
1924 (CR 469, Red, Yellow and
Black Streak)

168

Appendix II

Works Given to Institutions
During the Artist's Lifetime

Works are listed alphabetically by name of institution and year of gift. If gifts exceed one in a single year, they are listed alphabetically by title, followed in parentheses by date of work and corresponding catalogue raisonné entry number. Titles of works correspond to those in the catalogue raisonné.

The Art Institute of Chicago (7)

1947

Cow's Skull with Calico Roses (1931, CR 772)

1955

Red and Pink Rocks and Teeth (1938, CR 945)

1956

Green Mountains, Canada (1932, CR 818)

1965

Yellow Hickory Leaves with Daisy (1928, CR 642)

1969

The Black Place (1943, CR 1058)

Blue and Green Music (1921, CR 344)

1983

Sky Above Clouds IV (1965, CR 1498)

The Carl Van Vechten Gallery of Fine Arts, Fisk University, Nashville, Tennessee (2)

1950

Flying Backbone (1944, CR 1079)

1957

Radiator Bldg – Night, New York (1927, CR 577)

The Metropolitan Museum of Art, New York (13)

1950

Corn Dark (1924, CR 455)

No. 13 Special (1916/17, CR 157)

1952

Cow's Skull, Red, White and Blue (1931, CR 773)

1959

Black Place II (1944, CR 1081)

From the Faraway Nearby (Deer's Horns, Near Cameron) (1937, CR 914)

1961

Ranchos Church (1930, CR 704)

1962

Clam Shell (1930, CR 707)

1963

Near Abiquiu, N. M. 2 (1930, CR 735)

1964

White Canadian Barn, No. 2 (1932, CR 807)

1969

Abstraction (1916, CR 99)

Black Abstraction (1927, CR 574)

Black Iris (1926, CR 557)

Blue Lines (1916, CR 64)

Philadelphia Museum of Art (1)

1949

Red Hills and Bones (1941, CR 1025)

Appendix III

Works Named as Bequests in
O'Keeffe's 1979 Will

Works are listed alphabetically by
name of institution, then alphabetically by title, followed in
parentheses by corresponding catalogue raisonné entry number.
Titles are listed as recorded in the
catalogue raisonné; works that
were subsequently sold are indicated by referring the reader to
Lynes's essay, note 59.

The Art Institute of Chicago (9)

Ballet Skirt or Electric Light
(1927, CR 601)

*Black Rock with Blue Sky and
White Clouds* (1972, CR 1580)

Cliffs Beyond Abiquiu (1943,
could not be identified)

From a Day with Juan IV
(1976/77, CR 1627)

It Was Yellow and Pink III (1960,
CR 1442)

Pelvis III (1944, CR 1077, see
note 59)

Sky Above Clouds IV (1965,
CR 1498, see note 59)

White Patio with Red Door (1960,
CR 1445, see note 59)

White Shell with Red (c. 1938,
CR 958)

Brooklyn Museum of Art (6)

Dark Tree Trunks (1946,
CR 1152)

Fishhook from Hawaii – No. 1
(1939, CR 960)

Green Yellow and Orange (1960,
CR 1441)

Red Hills with the Pedernal
(1936, CR 898)

Rib and Jawbone (1935, CR 853)

2 Yellow Leaves (1928, CR 640)

The Cleveland Museum of Art (5)

*Cliffs Beyond Abiquiu – Dry
Waterfall* (1943, CR 1061)

Dead Tree with Pink Hill (1945,
CR 1118)

It Was Yellow and Pink II (1959,
CR 1355)

Sunflower, New Mexico I (1935,
CR 867)

White Pansy (1927, CR 590)

The Metropolitan Museum of Art, New York (4)

*Grey Line with Lavender and
Yellow* (1923/24, CR 442)

Grey Tree, Lake George (1925,
CR 512)

*Red and Yellow Cliffs Ghost
Ranch* (1940, CR 997)

River, New York (1928, CR 619)

Museum of Fine Arts, Boston (9)

A Sunflower from Maggie (1937,
CR 922)

D. H. Lawrence Pine Tree (1929,
CR 687, see note 59)

Fishhook from Hawaii, No. 2
(1939, CR 961)

Grey Wash Forms (1936, CR 897)

*Shell and Old Shingle IV / Shell
and Old Shingle No. 4* (1926,
CR 543)

*Shell and Old Shingle I / Shell
and Old Shingle No. I* (1926,
CR 540)

*Shell & Old Shingle III / Shell and
Old Shingle No. 3* (1926, CR 542)

*Shell & Old Shingle II / Shell and
Old Shingle No. II* (1926, CR 541)

Shell & Shingle Series VII (1926,
CR 546)

The Museum of Modern Art, New York (4)

An Orchid (1941, CR 1017)

Black Door with Snow (1955,
CR 1279, see note 59)

Ladder to the Moon (1958,
CR 1335, see note 59)

Summer Days (1936, CR 880,
see note 59)

National Gallery of Art, Washington, DC (10)

Black and White (1930, CR 700,
see note 59)

Cow's Skull on Red (1931/36,
CR 799, see note 59)

Jack-in-Pulpit – No. 2 (1930,
CR 716)

Jack-in-the-Pulpit No. 3 (1930,
CR 717)

Jack-in-the-Pulpit No. IV (1930,
CR 718)

Jack-in-Pulpit Abstraction – No. 5
(1930, CR 719)

Jack-in-the-Pulpit No. VI (1930,
CR 720)

Line and Curve (1927, CR 572)

Shell No. I (1928, CR 622)

Sky with Flat White Cloud (1962,
CR 1473)

Philadelphia Museum of Art (4)

Birch and Pine Tree No. 1 (1925,
CR 507)

From the Lake, No. 3 (1924,
CR 471)

Red & Orange Streak / Streak
(1919, CR 287)

2 Calla Lilies on Pink (1928,
CR 629)

Appendix IV

Works on Paper and Canvas
Owned by the Artist at the
Time of Her Death

Works are listed chronologically by date, then alphabetically by title, followed in parentheses by name of current owner and corresponding catalogue raisonné entry number. If no owner is indicated, the work remains with The Georgia O'Keeffe Foundation. Titles of works correspond to those in the catalogue raisonné.

1915

Early Abstraction (Milwaukee Art Museum, Milwaukee, Wisconsin, CR 50)

Early No. 2 (The Menil Collection, Houston, CR 51)

No. 5 Special (National Gallery of Art, Washington, DC, CR 46)

No. 4 Special (National Gallery of Art, CR 49)

No. 7 Special (National Gallery of Art, CR 47)

No. 32 – Special (National Museum of American Art, Washington, DC, CR 57)

No. 3 – Special (National Gallery of Art, CR 48)

No. 12 – Special (National Gallery of Art, CR 52)

No. 20 – From Music – Special (National Gallery of Art, CR 53)

No. 2 – Special (National Gallery of Art, CR 45)

Second, Out of My Head (National Gallery of Art, CR 56)

Untitled (Amon Carter Museum, Fort Worth, Texas, CR 55)

c. 1915/16

Abstraction with Curve and Circle (Georgia O'Keeffe Museum, Santa Fe, New Mexico, CR 60)

Drawing (CR 59)

1916

Anything (CR 90)

Blue Hill No. I (CR 108)

Evening (Georgia O'Keeffe Museum, CR 104)

First Drawing of the Blue Lines (National Gallery of Art, CR 62)

Inside the Tent While at U. of Virginia (CR 115)

Morning Sky with Houses (CR 127)

No. 14 Special (National Gallery of Art, CR 61)

No. 12 Special (The Museum of Modern Art, New York, CR 117)

I – Special (National Gallery of Art, CR 116)

Pink and Blue Mountain (Georgia O'Keeffe Museum, CR 106)

Sunrise and Little Clouds No. II (Georgia O'Keeffe Museum, CR 134)

Untitled (Abstraction) (CR 121)

Untitled (Abstraction / New York) (CR 65)

Untitled (Boy) (CR 100)

Untitled (Girl) (CR 101)

Untitled (Houses and Landscape) (CR 96)

Untitled (Tent Door at Night) (CR 112)

Untitled (Windmill) (private foundation, CR 122)

Untitled (Windmills) (private foundation, CR 123)

1916/17

No. 15 Special (Philadelphia Museum of Art, CR 154)

No. 20 – Special (Milwaukee Art Museum, CR 156)

No. 24 – Special / No. 24 (CR 166)

No. 21 – Special (Museum of Fine Arts, Museum of New Mexico, Santa Fe, CR 155)

No. 22 – Special (Georgia O'Keeffe Museum, CR 160)

Red Landscape (Panhandle – Plains Historical Museum, Canyon, Texas, CR 159)

Untitled (Abstraction) (National Gallery of Art, CR 158)

c. 1916/17

Untitled (Woman in Blue Dress) (private collection, CR 172)

1917

Canyon with Crows (private collection, CR 197)

Church Bell, Ward, Colorado (CR 213)

Evening Star No. IV (private collection, CR 202)

Evening Star No. VI (Georgia O'Keeffe Museum, CR 204)

Nude No. I (CR 176)

Nude No. VI (CR 183)

Nude No. III (National Gallery of Art, CR 187)

Nude Series (Georgia O'Keeffe Museum, CR 186)

Nude Series, VIII (Georgia O'Keeffe Museum, CR 182)

Nude Series IX (CR 178)

Nude Series VII (Georgia O'Keeffe Museum, CR 181)

Nude Series XII (Georgia O'Keeffe Museum, CR 188)

Nude Series II (CR 177)

Portrait – W – No. III (Georgia O'Keeffe Museum, CR 194)

Red Mesa (private collection, CR 198)

Starlight Night (private collection, CR 207)

Untitled (Colorado Landscape) (private collection, CR 218)

Untitled (Long Lake, Colorado) (Gerald Peters Gallery, Santa Fe, New Mexico, CR 219)

Yellow House (Gerald and Kathleen Peters, Santa Fe, New Mexico, CR 174)

1918

Blue Flower (Juan and Anna Maria Hamilton, CR 259)

Figure in Black (private foundation, CR 235)

Figures under Rooftop (Georgia O'Keeffe Museum, CR 229)

House with Picket Fence (private collection, CR 231)

House with Tree – Green (CR 232)

House with Tree – Red (Museum of Fine Arts, Museum of New Mexico, CR 233)

No. 16 Special (National Gallery of Art, CR 251)

Old Tree (CR 265)

Over Blue (private collection, CR 256)

Series 1, No. 4 (Städtische Galerie im Lenbachhaus, Munich, CR 255)

Series I – No. 3 (Milwaukee Art Museum, CR 254)

Series I – No. 2 (Milwaukee Art Museum, CR 262)

Three Women (Georgia O'Keeffe Museum, CR 237)

Untitled (Bowl of Fruit) (Georgia O'Keeffe Museum, CR 244)

Untitled (Leah) (Sheldon Memorial Art Gallery, University of Nebraska – Lincoln, CR 242)

Untitled (Old Tree) (private collection, CR 263)

Untitled (Old Tree) (Bebe and Crosby Kemper Private Collection, Kansas City, Missouri, CR 264)

Untitled (Tree with Green Shade) (private foundation, CR 228)

Untitled (Woman with Black Shawl) (CR 238)

Window – Red and Blue Sill (Georgia O'Keeffe Museum, CR 230)

Woman with Apron (Georgia O'Keeffe Museum, CR 236)

Woman with Blue Shawl (private foundation, CR 239)

1919

Blue Line (Georgia O'Keeffe Museum, CR 294)

Blue Shapes (Juan and Anna Maria Hamilton, CR 278)

Crazy Day (National Gallery of Art, CR 277)

Drawing 18 – Special (Amon Carter Museum, Fort Worth, Texas, CR 307)

Green Lines and Pink (Georgia O'Keeffe Museum, CR 282)

Lake George, Coat and Red (The Museum of Modern Art, CR 289)

No. 17 – Special (Georgia O'Keeffe Museum, CR 280)

Red & Orange Streak / Streak (Philadelphia Museum of Art, CR 287)

Series I, No. 8 (Städtische Galerie im Lenbachhaus, Munich, CR 293)

Series I, No. 7 (Milwaukee Art Museum, CR 279)

Series I, No. 10 (CR 291)

Series I – No. 10 A (CR 290)

Series I White & Blue Flower Shapes (CR 292)

Special No. 39 (The Museum of Modern Art, CR 281)

1920

Abstraction Seaweed and Water – Maine (CR 326)

Apple Family – 2 (Georgia O'Keeffe Museum, CR 315)

Series I, No. 12 (Georgia O'Keeffe Museum, CR 311)

Tree with Cut Limb (CR 327)

c. 1920

Untitled (Lake George Landscape) (Milwaukee Art Museum, CR 331, verso of CR 279)

1920/21

Alligator Pear – No. 2 (CR 337)

Alligator Pears (CR 338)

Trees in Autumn (Georgia O'Keeffe Museum, CR 341)

1921

Abstraction of Stream (Juan and Anna Maria Hamilton, CR 342)

Apple Family 3 (Milwaukee Art Museum, CR 347)

Cow Licking (The Denver Art Museum, CR 346)

Flower and Vase (private collection, CR 354)

Lake George with Crows (National Gallery of Canada, Ottawa, CR 358)

3 Zinnias (CR 353)

Water Lily (CR 350)

1922

Red Maple (CR 399)

Starlight Night, Lake George (private collection, CR 393)

1923

Alligator Pears (CR 417)

Calla Lily – Tall Glass – No. 1 (private collection, CR 425)

Calla Lily in Tall Glass – No. 2 (Georgia O'Keeffe Museum, CR 426)

Calla Lily Turned Away (Georgia O'Keeffe Museum, CR 423)

c. 1923

Untitled (Alligator Pear in Red Dish) (private collection, CR 439)

1923/24

Grey Line with Lavender and Yellow (The Metropolitan Museum of Art, New York, CR 442)

1924

A Celebration (Seattle Art Museum, CR 452)

Calla Lilies (private collection, CR 459)

The Chestnut Red (The R. Crosby Kemper Charitable Foundations, Kansas City, Missouri, CR 472)

Corn, No. 2 (Georgia O'Keeffe Museum, CR 454)

From the Lake, No. 3 (Philadelphia Museum of Art, CR 471)

From the Old Garden, No. 2 (private collection, CR 457)

Portrait of a Day – First Day (Spencer Museum of Art, The University of Kansas, CR 448)

Portrait of a Day – Second Day (Spencer Museum of Art, The University of Kansas, CR 449)

Red, Yellow and Black Streak (Musée national d'art moderne, Centre Georges Pompidou, Paris, CR 469)

1925

Birch and Pine Tree No. 1 (Philadelphia Museum of Art, CR 507)

Birch and Pine Tree, No. 2 (Rahr-West Art Museum, Manitowoc, Wisconsin, CR 508)

Canna Leaves (Georgia O'Keeffe Museum, CR 503)

Grey Tree, Lake George (The Metropolitan Museum of Art, CR 512)

Petunias (Fine Arts Museums of San Francisco, CR 491)

1926

Clam and Mussel (CR 534)

Shell and Old Shingle IV / Shell and Old Shingle No. 4 (Museum of Fine Arts, Boston, CR 543)

Shell and Old Shingle I / Shell and Old Shingle No. I (Museum of Fine Arts, Boston, CR 540)

Shell & Shingle Series VII (Museum of Fine Arts, Boston, CR 546)

Shell & Old Shingle III / Shell and Old Shingle No. 3 (Museum of Fine Arts, Boston, CR 542)

Shell & Old Shingle II / Shell and Old Shingle No. II (Museum of Fine Arts, Boston, CR 541)

Tan Clam Shell with Seaweed (CR 535)

White Flowers (University Art Museum, The University of New Mexico, Albuquerque, CR 549)

c. 1926

Untitled (Tulip) (Brooklyn Museum of Art, New York, CR 570, verso of CR 853)

1927

Abstraction White Rose (Georgia O'Keeffe Museum, CR 599)

Ballet Skirt or Electric Light (The Art Institute of Chicago, CR 601)

Calla Lily for Alfred (Georgia O'Keeffe Museum, CR 587)

Dark Iris No. III (Georgia O'Keeffe Museum, CR 602)

Grapes on White Plate (private collection, CR 579)

Lake George Autumn (Milwaukee Art Museum, CR 607)

Line and Curve (National Gallery of Art, CR 572)

Seaweed (Iris & B. Gerald Cantor Center for Visual Arts at Stanford University, Palo Alto, California, CR 604)

White Calla Lily (private collection, CR 586)

White Pansy (The Cleveland Museum of Art, CR 590)

c. 1927

Untitled (Skunk Cabbage) (private collection, CR 613)

1928

Abstraction No. VI (private collection, CR 615)

Calla Lilies on Red (Georgia O'Keeffe Museum, CR 628)

Last Yellow White Birch (private collection, CR 645)

River, New York (The Metropolitan Museum of Art, CR 619)

Shell No. I (National Gallery of Art, CR 622)

2 Calla Lilies on Pink (Philadelphia Museum of Art, CR 629)

2 Yellow Leaves (Brooklyn Museum of Art, CR 640)

1928/29

3 Eggs in Pink Dish (Museum of Fine Arts, Museum of New Mexico, CR 647)

1929

Grey and Brown Leaves (Milwaukee Art Museum, CR 676)

Grey Blue & Black – Pink Circle (Dallas Museum of Art, CR 651)

Pink Dish and Green Leaves (private collection, CR 654)

The Wooden Virgin (private collection, CR 673)

1930

Jack-in-Pulpit Abstraction – No. 5 (National Gallery of Art, CR 719)

Jack-in-the-Pulpit No. IV (National Gallery of Art, CR 718)

Jack-in-the-Pulpit No. VI (National Gallery of Art, CR 720)

Jack-in-Pulpit – No. 3 (National Gallery of Art, CR 717)

Jack-in-Pulpit – No. 2 (National Gallery of Art, CR 716)

Mountain at Bear Lake – Taos (The White House, Washington, DC, CR 744)

1931

Dark & Lavender Leaves (Museum of Fine Arts, Museum of New Mexico, CR 787)

Horse's Skull with Pink Rose (Los Angeles County Museum of Art, CR 775)

Paul's Kachina (CR 782)

1932

East River (CR 802)

Manhattan (National Museum of American Art, CR 801)

Nature Forms – Gaspé (private collection, CR 819)

Untitled (New York) (CR 803)

1934

Banyan Tree (CR 839)

Kachina (Georgia O'Keeffe Museum, CR 823)

Kachina (Georgia O'Keeffe Museum, CR 824)

Small Purple Hills (private collection, CR 838)

Special No. 40 (Philadelphia Museum of Art, CR 821)

Untitled (Banyan Tree) (CR 840)

Untitled (Banyan Tree) (CR 841)

Untited (Banyan Tree) (CR 845)

1935

Horseshoe with Feather No. I (CR 857)

Kachina with Horns from Back (private collection, CR 858)

Rib and Jawbone (Brooklyn Museum of Art, CR 853)

Sunflower, New Mexico I (The Cleveland Museum of Art, CR 867)

Untitled (Kachina with Horns) (Gerald Peters Gallery, Santa Fe, New Mexico, CR 859)

Turkey Feather with Horseshoe, II (CR 856)

Turkey Feathers in Indian Pot (private collection, CR 855)

Yellow Cactus (private collection, CR 869)

c. 1935

Untitled (Abstraction) (CR 873)

1936

Grey Hill Forms (Museum of Fine Arts, Museum of New Mexico, CR 895)

Grey Wash Forms (Museum of Fine Arts, Boston, CR 897)

Horizontal Horse's or Mule's Skull with Feather (Milwaukee Art Museum, CR 878)

Jonquils I (private collection, CR 887)

Red Hills with the Pedernal (Brooklyn Museum of Art, CR 898)

Yellow Jonquils No. III (The Enid and Crosby Kemper Foundation, Kansas City, Missouri, CR 889)

c. 1936

Untitled (Ghost Ranch Landscape) (Georgia O'Keeffe Museum, CR 910)

1937

A Sunflower from Maggie (Museum of Fine Arts, Boston, CR 922)

Chama River, Ghost Ranch (Museum of Fine Arts, Museum of New Mexico, CR 933)

Hollyhock Pink with the Pedernal, New Mexico (private collection, CR 924)

Hollyhock White with Pedernal (The National Museum of Modern Art, Tokyo, CR 923)

Horn and Feathers (CR 916)

Part of the Cliffs (private collection, CR 931)

Red Hills and White Flower (Georgia O'Keeffe Museum, CR 925)

Two Pink Shells / Pink Shell (Georgia O'Keeffe Museum, CR 920)

1938

The Cliff Chimneys (Milwaukee Art Museum, CR 955)

Dead Cedar Stump (University Art Museum, The University of New Mexico, CR 956)

Geranium Leaves in Pink Dish (CR 953)

c. 1938

White Shell with Red (The Art Institute of Chicago, CR 958)

1939

Black Lava Bridge, Hāna Coast, No. I (Honolulu Academy of Arts, CR 976)

Black Lava Bridge, Hāna Coast – No. 2 (Honolulu Academy of Arts, CR 977)

Fishhook from Hawaii – No. 1 (Brooklyn Museum of Art, CR 960)

Fishhook from Hawaii, No. 2 (Museum of Fine Arts, Boston, CR 961)

Papaw Tree, 'Iao Valley, Maui (Honolulu Academy of Arts, CR 982)

Untitled (Hibiscus) (CR 970)

1930s

Untitled (Yellow Flower) (CR 984)

1940

Dorothy Schubart (CR 989)

The Patio – No. I (private collection, CR 986)

Red and Yellow Cliffs Ghost Ranch (The Metropolitan Museum of Art, CR 997)

1941

A Man from the Desert (CR 1015)

From a New Jersey Weekend I (private collection, CR 1011)

From a New Jersey Weekend II (The Art Museum, Princeton University, Princeton, New Jersey, CR 1012)

Mariposa Lilies and Indian Paintbrush (CR 1016)

My Front Yard, Summer (CR 1023)

An Orchid (The Museum of
Modern Art, CR 1017)

Pedernal (CR 1022)

Road to Pedernal (CR 1020)

Untitled (Pedernal) (CR 1021)

White Feather (CR 1013)

1941/42

Pedernal (Georgia O'Keeffe
Museum, CR 1029)

1942

Feathers, White and Grey
(CR 1033)

Kokopelli (CR 1035)

Kokopelli with Snow (Georgia
O'Keeffe Museum, CR 1036)

1943

*Cliffs Beyond Abiquiu – Dry
Waterfall* (The Cleveland Museum
of Art, CR 1061)

Dead Piñon Tree (CR 1068)

Horns (CR 1054)

Untitled (Abstraction) (CR 1051)

Untitled (Beauford Delaney)
(CR 1041)

Untitled (Beauford Delaney)
(Philadelphia Museum of Art,
CR 1043)

Untitled (Beauford Delaney)
(CR 1044)

c. 1943

*Untitled (Dry Waterfall, Ghost
Ranch)* (Georgia O'Keeffe
Museum, CR 1071)

Untitled (Ghost Ranch Cliff)
(Georgia O'Keeffe Museum,
CR 1070)

Untitled (New Mexico Landscape)
(CR 1072)

Untitled (New Mexico Landscape)
(CR 1073)

1944

Black Place III (private foundation, CR 1082)

Cottonwood I (private foundation,
CR 1084)

Pelvis IV (Georgia O'Keeffe
Museum, CR 1078)

c. 1944/45

Abiquiu Mesa I (Georgia O'Keeffe
Museum, CR 1091)

Abiquiu Mesa II (Georgia O'Keeffe
Museum, CR 1092)

1945

Abstraction (CR 1102)

Dead Tree with Pink Hill (The
Cleveland Museum of Art,
CR 1118)

Pedernal (Georgia O'Keeffe
Museum, CR 1117)

Spring Tree No. I (Museum of Fine
Arts, Museum of New Mexico,
CR 1120)

Untitled (Cottonwood Tree)
(CR 1119)

1946

Dark Tree Trunks (Brooklyn
Museum of Art, CR 1152)

Part of the Cliff (CR 1150)

1948

Cottonwood and Pedernal
(CR 1165)

In the Patio V (Museo de Arte
Contemporaneo Internacional
Rufino Tamayo/CNCA – CONA-
CULTA, Mexico, CR 1162)

In the Patio III (CR 1160)

c. 1949

Ram's Horns I (CR 1176)

1950

Cottonwoods Near Abiquiu
(CR 1216)

*Early Spring Trees above Irrigation
Ditch, Abiquiu* (CR 1219)

In the Patio VIII (Georgia O'Keeffe
Museum, CR 1211)

In the Patio IX (private collection,
CR 1213)

Winter Trees, Abiquiu, I (private
collection, CR 1218)

Winter Trees, Abiquiu, III
(CR 1220)

175

1952

Ghost Ranch Cliff (private collection, CR 1236)

Lavender Hill with Green (Georgia
O'Keeffe Museum, CR 1233)

Mesa and Road East (CR 1234)

Mesa and Road East II (CR 1235)

c. 1952

Cottonwoods (CR 1261)

1953

Easter Sunrise (CR 1266)

Green Tree (CR 1268)

1954

Winter Cottonwoods East IV
(CR 1275)

1955

Black Door with Snow
(Eugene and Clare Thaw, Santa Fe,
New Mexico, CR 1279)

1956

Door Through Window (CR 1293)

Patio Door with Green Leaf
(Georgia O'Keeffe Museum,
CR 1292)

1957

Machu Pichu I (CR 1318)

Misti – A Memory (CR 1319)

Misti Again – A Memory (Georgia
O'Keeffe Museum, CR 1321)

Untitled (Misti – A Memory)
(private collection, CR 1320)

Untitled (Sacsayhuaman)
(CR 1310)

c. 1957

Rose (CR 1327)

1957/58

Green and White (Georgia
O'Keeffe Museum, CR 1329)

1958

Blue II (Georgia O'Keeffe
Museum, CR 1331)

1959

Another Drawing Similar
Shape (Milwaukee Art Museum,
CR 1341)

Blue – A (CR 1356)

Drawing V (Georgia O'Keeffe
Museum, CR 1339)

Drawing IX (CR 1348)

Drawing III (Philadelphia Museum
of Art, CR 1351)

Drawing II (CR 1346)

From the River – Pale (CR 1360)

It Was Yellow and Pink II
(The Cleveland Museum of Art,
CR 1355)

Untitled (Road) (private collection, CR 1368)

1959/60

Tan, Orange, Yellow,
Lavender (Georgia O'Keeffe
Museum, CR 1417)

1960

Green Yellow and Orange
(Brooklyn Museum of Art,
CR 1441)

It Was Yellow and Pink III (The Art
Institute of Chicago, CR 1442)

Untitled (Mt. Fuji) (CR 1446)

Untitled (Mt. Fuji) (Georgia
O'Keeffe Museum, CR 1447)

1960/64

Sky Above the Flat White Cloud II
(CR 1460)

1961

Mountains and Lake (CR 1462)

1962

An Island with Clouds (CR 1472)

Blue Road (private collection,
CR 1471)

Sky with Flat White Cloud
(National Gallery of Art, CR 1473)

1962/63

Above the Clouds I (Georgia
O'Keeffe Museum, CR 1474)

1963

Winter Road I (National Gallery of
Art, CR 1477)

1963/64

Clouds 5 / Yellow Horizon and
Clouds (CR 1484)

1963/71

Untitled (Black Rock with White
Background (CR 1485)

1964

On the River (Museum of Fine
Arts, Museum of New Mexico,
CR 1486)

c. 1965

Canyon Country (Phoenix Art
Museum, Phoenix, Arizona,
CR 1504)

Canyon Country, White and Brown
Cliffs (CR 1501)

Canyon No. II (CR 1502)

On the River I (CR 1503)

1960s

Idol (CR 1514)

Idol's Head (CR 1515)

1970

Black Rock with Blue III (private
collection, CR 1578)

1971

Black Rock on Red (Georgia
O'Keeffe Museum, CR 1579)

1972

The Beyond (CR 1581)

Black Rock with Blue Sky and
White Clouds (The Art Institute of
Chicago, CR 1580)

1976

Branches with Sun (CR 1607)

Palm Tree (CR 1602)

Palm Tree at My Door – Antigua
(CR 1604)

Redwoods Big Sur (CR 1609)

Untitled (Redwoods Big Sur)
(CR 1608)

Untitled (Trees) (CR 1600)

1976/77

From a Day at Esther's (CR 1612)

From a Day with Juan A
(CR 1628)

From a Day with Juan IV (The Art
Institute of Chicago, CR 1627)

From a Day with Juan II (The
Museum of Modern Art, CR 1626)

Sky Above Clouds / Yellow Horizon
and Clouds (CR 1618)

Untitled (Abstraction Blue Circle
and Line) (CR 1611)

Untitled (Abstraction Pink and
Green) (CR 1613)

Untitled (Curved Line and Round
Spots – Blue) (CR 1614)

Untitled (From a Day with Juan)
(CR 1623)

Untitled (From a Day with Juan)
(CR 1629)

Untitled (From a Day with Juan)
(private collection, CR 1630)

Untitled (From a Day with Juan)
(CR 1631)

Untitled (From a Day with Juan
III) (CR 1625)

Appendix V

Works Distributed by The
Georgia O'Keeffe Foundation
Since 1986

Works are listed chronologically
by date of gift, then alphabetically
by name of institution. If gifts
exceed one in a single year, they
are listed alphabetically by title
followed in parentheses by date of
work and corresponding catalogue
raisonné number. Titles correspond to those in the catalogue
raisonné.

1987 Gifts

**Museum of Fine Arts, Museum of
New Mexico, Santa Fe (1)**

3 Eggs in Pink Dish (1928/29,
CR 647)

**University Art Museum,
University of New Mexico,
Albuquerque (3)**

Dead Cedar Stump (1938,
CR 956)

Grey Hill Forms (1936, CR 895)

White Flowers (1926, CR 549)

1988 Gifts

**Museum of Fine Arts, Museum of
New Mexico (3)**

Chama River, Ghost Ranch (1937,
CR 933)

On the River (1964, CR 1486)

Spring Tree No. I (1945, CR 1120)

1992 Gifts

**National Gallery of Art,
Washington, DC (14)**

Crazy Day (1919, CR 277)

First Drawing of the Blue Lines
(1916, CR 62)

No. 5 Special (1915, CR 46)

No. 4 Special (1915, CR 49)

No. 14 Special (1916, CR 61)

No. 7 Special (1915, CR 47)

No. 16 Special (1918, CR 251)

No. 3 – Special (1915, CR 48)

No. 12 – Special (1915, CR 52)

No. 20 – From Music – Special
(1915, CR 53)

No. 2 – Special (1915 CR 45)

I – Special (1916, CR 116)

Second, Out of My Head (1915,
CR 56)

Untitled (Abstraction) (1916/17,
CR 158)

1993 Gifts

**Museum of Fine Arts, Museum of
New Mexico (3)**

Dark & Lavender Leaves (1931,
CR 787)

House with Tree – Red (1918,
CR 233)

No. 21 – Special (1916/17,
CR 155)

1994 Gifts

**The Art Museum, Princeton
University, Princeton, New Jersey
(1)**

From a New Jersey Weekend II
(1941, CR 1012)

Dallas Museum of Art (1)

Grey Blue & Black – Pink Circle
(1929, CR 651)

Honolulu Academy of Arts (3)

Black Lava Bridge, Hāna Coast,
No. I (1939, CR 976)

Black Lava Bridge, Hāna Coast –
No. 2 (1939, CR 977)

Papaw Tree, 'Iao Valley, Maui
(1939, CR 982)

**Los Angeles County Museum of
Art (1)**

Horse's Skull with Pink Rose
(1931, CR 775)

**Milwaukee Art Museum,
Milwaukee, Wisconsin (1)**

Grey and Brown Leaves (1929,
CR 676)

**National Museum of Modern Art,
Tokyo (1)**

Hollyhock White with Pedernal
(1937, CR 923)

**Panhandle – Plains Historical
Museum, Canyon, Texas (1)**

Red Landscape (1916/17,
CR 159)

**Phoenix Art Museum, Phoenix,
Arizona (1)**

Canyon Country (c. 1965,
CR 1504)

**Seattle Art Museum, Seattle,
Washington (1)**

A Celebration (1924, CR 452)

**Spencer Museum of Art,
The University of Kansas,
Lawrence (2)**

Portrait of a Day – First Day
(1924, CR 448)

Portrait of a Day – Second Day
(1924, CR 449)

1995 Gifts

**The Menil Collection,
Houston (1)**

Early No. 2 (1915, CR 51)

**Musée national d'art moderne,
Centre Georges Pompidou,
Paris (1)**

Red, Yellow and Black Streak
(1924, CR 469)

**Museo de Arte Contemporáneo
Internacional Rufino
Tamayo/CNCA –
CONACULTA, Mexico (1)**

In the Patio V (1948, CR 1162)

**The Museum of Modern Art,
New York (3)**

Lake George, Coat and Red
(1919, CR 289)

No. 12 Special (1916, CR 117)

Special No. 39 (1919, CR 281)

National Gallery of Art (1)

Winter Road I (1963, CR 1477)

**National Gallery of Canada,
Ottawa (1)**

Lake George with Crows (1921,
CR 358)

**National Museum of American
Art, Washington, DC (2)**

Manhattan (1932, CR 801)

No. 32 – Special (1915, CR 57)

Städtische Galerie im Lenbachhaus, Munich (2)

Series I, No. 8 (1919, CR 293)

Series 1, No. 4 (1918, CR 255)

1996 Gift/Purchase

National Gallery of Art (1)

Nude No. III (1917, CR 187)

1997 Gifts

Georgia O'Keeffe Museum (2)

Kachina (1934, CR 823)

Kachina (1934, CR 824)

1997 Gift/Purchases

Amon Carter Museum, Fort Worth, Texas (2)

Drawing 18 – Special (1919, CR 307)

Untitled (1915, CR 55)

Georgia O'Keeffe Museum (33)

Abiquiu Mesa I (c. 1944/45, CR 1091)

Abiquiu Mesa II (c. 1944/45, CR 1092)

Above the Clouds I (1962/63, CR 1474)

Abstraction (1946, cast 1979/80, CR 1141)

Abstraction White Rose (1927, CR 599)

Abstraction with Curve and Circle (c. 1915/16, CR 60)

Apple Family – 2 (1920, CR 315)

Black Rock on Red (1971, CR 1579)

Blue Line (1919, CR 294)

Blue II (1958, CR 1331)

Corn, No. 2 (1924, CR 454)

Dark Iris No. III (1927, CR 602)

Drawing V (1959, CR 1339)

Evening (1916, CR 104)

Green and White (1957/58, CR 1329)

Green Lines and Pink (1919, CR 282)

In the Patio VIII (1950, CR 1211)

Kokopelli with Snow (1942, CR 1036)

Lavender Hill with Green (1952, CR 1233)

Misti Again – A Memory (1957, CR 1321)

Nude Series (1917, CR 186)

Nude Series, VIII (1917, CR 182)

Nude Series VII (1917, CR 181)

Nude Series XII (1917, CR 188)

No. 17 – Special (1919, CR 280)

No. 22 – Special (1916/17, CR 160)

Patio Door with Green Leaf (1956, CR 1292)

Pedernal (1941/42, CR 1029)

Pink and Blue Mountain (1916, CR 106)

Portrait – W – No. III (1917, CR 194)

Series I, No. 12 (1920, CR 311)

Tan, Orange, Yellow, Lavender (1959/60, CR 1417)

Two Pink Shells / Pink Shell (1937, CR 920)

Iris & B. Gerald Cantor Center for Visual Arts at Stanford University, Palo Alto, California (1)

Seaweed (1927, CR 604)

Milwaukee Art Museum (7)

Another Drawing Similar Shape (1959, CR 1341)

Early Abstraction (1915, CR 50)

No. 20 – Special (1916/17, CR, 156)

Series I, No. 7 (1919, CR 279)

Series I – No. 3 (1918, CR 254)

Series I – No. 2 (1918 CR 262)

Untitled (Lake George Landscape) (c. 1920, CR 331, verso of CR 279)

Philadelphia Museum of Art (4)

Drawing III (1959, CR 1351)

No. 15 Special (1916/17, CR 154)

Special No. 40 (1934, CR 821)

Untitled (Beauford Delaney) (1943, CR 1043)

The White House, Washington, DC (1)

Mountain at Bear Lake – Taos (1930, CR 744)

1998 Gift/Purchases

Milwaukee Art Museum (4)

Apple Family 3 (1921, CR 347)

The Cliff Chimneys (1938, CR 955)

Horizontal Horse's or Mule's Skull with Feather (1936, CR 878)

Lake George Autumn (1927, CR 607)

Catalogue of the Exhibition

Works Owned by the Artist at the Time of Her Death or Given to Museums During Her Lifetime

The exhibition is organized thematically with variations in chronology following the order of the plates. "CR" refers to the O'Keeffe catalogue raisonné number.

The Early Years 1915–18

Pastels, Charcoals, and Sculpture, 1915–16

1
No. 32–Special
1915
Pastel on paper
14 ½ x 20 inches
National Museum of American Art, Smithsonian Institution, Washington, DC, Gift of The Georgia O'Keeffe Foundation
CR 57

2
No. 20–From Music–Special
1915
Charcoal on paper
13 ½ x 11 inches
National Gallery of Art, Washington, DC, Alfred Stieglitz Collection, Gift of The Georgia O'Keeffe Foundation (exhibited only at the Georgia O'Keeffe Museum)
CR 53

3
Early Abstraction
1915
Charcoal on paper
23 ³/₄ x 18 ³/₈ inches
Milwaukee Art Museum, Milwaukee, Wisconsin, Gift of Jane Bradley Pettit Foundation and The Georgia O'Keeffe Foundation
CR 50

4
First Drawing of the Blue Lines
1916
Charcoal on paper
24 ³/₄ x 18 ⁷/₈ inches
National Gallery of Art, Washington, DC, Alfred Stieglitz Collection, Gift of The Georgia O'Keeffe Foundation (exhibited only at the Milwaukee Art Museum)
CR 62

5
Abstraction
1916 (cast 1979/80)
White-lacquered bronze
10 x 10 x 1 ½ inches
The Georgia O'Keeffe Foundation, Abiquiu, New Mexico
CR 75

Watercolors, 1916–18

6
Sunrise and Little Clouds No. II
1916
Watercolor on paper
8 ⁷/₈ x 12 inches
Georgia O'Keeffe Museum, Santa Fe, New Mexico, Gift of The Burnett Foundation
CR 134

7
Morning Sky with Houses
1916
Watercolor and graphite on paper
8 ⁷/₈ x 12 inches
The Georgia O'Keeffe Foundation, Abiquiu, New Mexico
CR 127

8
Nude Series
1917
Watercolor on paper
12 x 8 ⁷/₈ inches
Georgia O'Keeffe Museum, Santa Fe, New Mexico, Gift of The Burnett Foundation and The Georgia O'Keeffe Foundation
CR 186

9
Evening Star No. VI
1917
Watercolor on paper
8 ⁷/₈ x 12 inches
Georgia O'Keeffe Museum, Santa Fe, New Mexico, Gift of The Burnett Foundation
CR 204

10
House with Tree–Red
1918
Watercolor on paper
16 x 11 inches
Museum of Fine Arts, Museum of New Mexico, Santa Fe, Gift of the Estate of Georgia O'Keeffe
CR 233

Palo Duro Canyon–Series

11
Untitled (Palo Duro Canyon)
1916/17
Graphite on paper
3 ⁷/₈ x 5 inches
The Georgia O'Keeffe Foundation, Abiquiu, New Mexico
CR 144

12
Untitled (Palo Duro Canyon)
1916/17
Graphite on paper
3 ⁷/₈ x 5 inches
The Georgia O'Keeffe Foundation, Abiquiu, New Mexico
CR 145

13
Untitled (Palo Duro Canyon)
1916/17
Graphite on paper
3 ⁷/₈ x 5 inches
The Georgia O'Keeffe Foundation, Abiquiu, New Mexico
CR 146

14
Untitled (Palo Duro Canyon)
1916/17
Graphite on paper
3 ⁷/₈ x 5 inches
The Georgia O'Keeffe Foundation, Abiquiu, New Mexico
CR 147

15
No. 20–Special
1916/17
Oil on board
17 ³/₈ x 13 ½ inches
Milwaukee Art Museum, Milwaukee, Wisconsin, Gift of Jane Bradley Pettit Foundation and The Georgia O'Keeffe Foundation
CR 156

16
No. 21–Special
1916/17
Oil on board
13 ½ x 16 ¼ inches
Museum of Fine Arts, Museum of New Mexico, Santa Fe, Gift of the Estate of Georgia O'Keeffe
CR 155

New York
1918–29

Abstractions – Series 1918–20

17
Series I – No. 2
1918
Oil on board
20 x 16 inches
Milwaukee Art Museum,
Milwaukee, Wisconsin, Gift of
Jane Bradley Pettit Foundation
and The Georgia O'Keeffe
Foundation
CR 262

18
Series I – No. 3
1918
Oil on board
20 x 16 inches
Milwaukee Art Museum,
Milwaukee, Wisconsin, Gift of
Jane Bradley Pettit Foundation
and The Georgia O'Keeffe
Foundation
CR 254

19
Series 1, No. 4
1918
Oil on canvas
20 x 16 inches
Städtische Galerie im
Lenbachhaus, Munich, Gift of
The Georgia O'Keeffe Foundation
CR 255

20
Series I, No. 7
1919
Oil on board
20 x 16 inches
Milwaukee Art Museum,
Milwaukee, Wisconsin, Gift of
Jane Bradley Pettit Foundation
and The Georgia O'Keeffe
Foundation
CR 279

21
Series I, No. 8
1919
Oil on canvas
20 x 16 inches
Städtische Galerie im
Lenbachhaus, Munich, Gift of
The Georgia O'Keeffe Foundation
CR 293

22
Series I, No. 12
1920
Oil on canvas
20 x 16 ¼ inches
Georgia O'Keeffe Museum,
Santa Fe, New Mexico, Gift of
The Burnett Foundation and The
Georgia O'Keeffe Foundation
CR 311

Abstractions, 1910s and 1920s

23
From the Lake, No. 3
1924
Oil on canvas
36 x 30 inches
Philadelphia Museum of Art:
Bequest of Georgia O'Keeffe for
the Alfred Stieglitz Collection
CR 471

24
Red, Yellow and Black Streak
1924
Oil on canvas
39 ⅜ x 31 ¾ inches
Musée national d'art moderne,
Centre Georges Pompidou, Paris.
Gift of The Georgia O'Keeffe
Foundation
CR 469

25
Grey Blue & Black – Pink Circle
1929
Oil on canvas
36 x 48 inches
Dallas Museum of Art, Gift of
The Georgia O'Keeffe Foundation
CR 651

Fruit and Shells

26
Apple Family – 2
1920
Oil on canvas
8 ⅛ x 10 ⅛ inches
Georgia O'Keeffe Museum,
Santa Fe, New Mexico, Gift of
The Burnett Foundation and The
Georgia O'Keeffe Foundation
CR 315

27
Apple Family 3
1921
Oil on canvas
7 ⅞ x 10 ⅞ inches
Milwaukee Art Museum,
Milwaukee, Wisconsin, Gift of

Jane Bradley Pettit Foundation
and The Georgia O'Keeffe
Foundation
CR 347

28
Tan Clam Shell with Seaweed
1926
Oil on canvas
9 x 7 inches
The Georgia O'Keeffe
Foundation, Abiquiu,
New Mexico
CR 535

29
Clam Shell
1930
Oil on canvas
24 x 36 inches
The Metropolitan Museum of Art,
New York, Alfred Stieglitz
Collection
CR 707

30
Seaweed
1927
Oil on canvas
9 x 7 inches
Iris & B. Gerald Cantor Center for
Visual Arts at Stanford
University; Gift of The Georgia
O'Keeffe Foundation, an anony-
mous donor, and the Committee
for Art Acquisitions Fund
CR 604

Leaves

31
Canna Leaves
1925
Oil on canvas
26 x 11 inches
Georgia O'Keeffe Museum,
Santa Fe, New Mexico, Gift of
The Burnett Foundation
CR 503

32
2 Yellow Leaves
1928
Oil on canvas
40 x 30 ⅛ inches
Brooklyn Museum of Art,
New York, Bequest of Georgia
O'Keeffe
CR 640

33
Dark & Lavender Leaves
1931
Oil on canvas
20 x 17 inches
Museum of Fine Arts, Museum of
New Mexico, Santa Fe, Gift of the
Estate of Georgia O'Keeffe
CR 787

34
Grey and Brown Leaves
1929
Oil on canvas
36 x 30 inches
Milwaukee Art Museum,
Milwaukee, Wisconsin, Gift of
The Georgia O'Keeffe Foundation
CR 676

Trees

35
Birch and Pine Tree, No. 2
1925
Oil on canvas
36 x 22 inches
Rahr-West Art Museum,
Manitowoc, Wisconsin,
Ruth and John D. West Collection
CR 508

36
Last Yellow White Birch
1928
Oil on canvas
36 x 29 ¾ inches
Private collection, New York
CR 645

Lake George

37
Lake George with Crows
1921
Oil on canvas
28 ½ x 25 inches
National Gallery of Canada,
Ottawa, Gift of The Georgia
O'Keeffe Foundation,
Abiquiu, New Mexico
(exhibited only at the Georgia
O'Keeffe Museum)
CR 358

38
Corn, No. 2
1924
Oil on canvas
27 ¼ x 10 inches
Georgia O'Keeffe Museum,

Santa Fe, New Mexico, Gift of
The Burnett Foundation and The
Georgia O'Keeffe Foundation
CR 454

39
Lake George Autumn
1927
Oil on canvas
17 x 32 inches
Milwaukee Art Museum,
Milwaukee, Wisconsin, Gift of
Jane Bradley Pettit Foundation
and The Georgia O'Keeffe
Foundation
CR 607

Architecture

40
*Untitled (New York Street with
Moon)*
1925
Graphite on paper
11 x 8 ½ inches
The Georgia O'Keeffe
Foundation, Abiquiu,
New Mexico
CR 482

41
River, New York
1928
Oil on canvas
12 x 32 inches
The Metropolitan Museum of Art,
New York, Alfred Stieglitz
Collection, Bequest of Georgia
O'Keeffe
CR 619

Flower Series

42
Abstraction White Rose
1927
Oil on canvas
36 x 30 inches
Georgia O'Keeffe Museum,
Santa Fe, New Mexico, Gift of
The Burnett Foundation and The
Georgia O'Keeffe Foundation
CR 599

43
Jack-in-Pulpit No. 1
1930
Oil on canvas
12 x 9 inches
Private collection, Courtesy Irene
Drori Inc., Los Angeles and
Santa Fe, New Mexico
CR 715

44
Jack-in-the-Pulpit No. 3
1930
Oil on canvas
40 x 30 inches
National Gallery of Art,
Washington, DC, Alfred Stieglitz
Collection, Bequest of Georgia
O'Keeffe
CR 717

45
Jack-in-the-Pulpit No. VI
1930
Oil on canvas
36 x 18 inches
National Gallery of Art,
Washington, DC, Alfred Steiglitz
Collection, Bequest of Georgia
O'Keeffe
CR 720

Flowers

46
White Pansy
1927
Oil on canvas
36 x 30 inches
The Cleveland Museum of Art,
Bequest of Georgia O'Keeffe
CR 590

47
2 Calla Lillies on Pink
1928
Oil on canvas
40 x 30 inches
Philadelphia Museum of Art,
Bequest of Georgia O'Keeffe for
the Alfred Stieglitz Collection
CR 629

48
A Sunflower from Maggie
1937
Oil on canvas
15 x 20 inches
Museum of Fine Arts, Boston,
Alfred Stieglitz Collection,
Bequest of Georgia O'Keeffe
CR 922

New Mexico
1929–84

Architecture

49
Ranchos Church
1929
Graphite on paper
8 ½ x 10 inches
The Georgia O'Keeffe
Foundation, Abiquiu,
New Mexico
CR 661

50
Ranchos Church
1930
Oil on canvas
24 x 36 inches
The Metropolitan Museum of Art,
New York, Alfred Stieglitz
Collection
CR 704

51
In the Patio VIII
1950
Oil on canvas
26 x 20 inches
Georgia O'Keeffe Museum,
Santa Fe, New Mexico, Gift of
The Burnett Foundation and The
Georgia O'Keeffe Foundation
CR 1211

52
Patio Door with Green Leaf
1956
Oil on canvas
36 x 30 inches
Georgia O'Keeffe Museum,
Santa Fe, New Mexico, Gift of
The Burnett Foundation and The
Georgia O'Keeffe Foundation
CR 1292

53
Black Door with Snow
1955
Oil on canvas
36 x 30 inches
Eugene and Clare Thaw,
Santa Fe, New Mexico
CR 1279

Still Life and Sculpture

54
Horse's Skull with Pink Rose
1931
Graphite on paper
10 x 8 ½ inches
The Georgia O'Keeffe
Foundation, Abiquiu,
New Mexico
CR 774

55
Horse's Skull with Pink Rose
1931
Oil on canvas
40 x 30 inches
Los Angeles County Museum of
Art, Gift of The Georgia O'Keeffe
Foundation
CR 775

56
Cow's Skull with Calico Roses
1931
Oil on canvas
36 x 24 inches
The Art Institute of Chicago,
Gift of Georgia O'Keeffe
CR 772

57
Turkey Feathers in Indian Pot
1935
Oil on canvas
24 x 8 ½ inches
Private collection, extended loan,
Elvehjem Museum of Art,
University of Wisconsin, Madison
CR 855

58
*Horizontal Horse's or Mule's
Skull with Feather*
1936
Oil on canvas
16 x 30 inches
Milwaukee Art Museum,
Milwaukee, Wisconsin, Gift of
Jane Bradley Pettit Foundation
and The Georgia O'Keeffe
Foundation
CR 878

59
Pelvis IV
1944
Oil on canvas
36 ⅛ x 48 ⅛ inches
Georgia O'Keeffe Museum,
Santa Fe, New Mexico, Gift of
The Burnett Foundation
CR 1078

60
Abstraction
1946 (cast 1979/80)
White-lacquered bronze
36 x 36 x 4 ½ inches
The Georgia O'Keeffe
Foundation, Abiquiu,
New Mexico
CR 1135

Landscape

61
Small Purple Hills
1934
Oil on board
16 x 19 ¾ inches
Collection of
June O'Keeffe Sebring
CR 838

62
Grey Wash Forms
1936
Oil on canvas
16 x 30 inches
Museum of Fine Arts, Boston,
Alfred Stieglitz Collection,
Bequest of Georgia O'Keeffe
CR 897

63
The Cliff Chimneys
1938
Oil on canvas
36 x 30 inches
Milwaukee Art Museum,
Milwaukee, Wisconsin, Gift of
Jane Bradley Pettit Foundation
and The Georgia O'Keeffe
Foundation
CR 955

64
Untitled (Red and Yellow Cliffs)
1940
Oil on canvas
24 x 36 inches
Georgia O'Keeffe Museum,
Santa Fe, New Mexico, Gift of
The Burnett Foundation
CR 998

65
*Untitled (Dry Waterfall, Ghost
Ranch)*
c. 1943
Graphite and charcoal on paper
22 ⅞ x 17 ⅞ inches
Georgia O'Keeffe Museum,
Santa Fe, New Mexico, Gift of
The Burnett Foundation
CR 1071

66
*Cliffs Beyond Abiquiu – Dry
Waterfall*
1943
Oil on canvas
30 x 16 inches
The Cleveland Museum of Art,
Bequest of Georgia O'Keeffe
CR 1061

67
Black Place III
1944
Oil on canvas
36 x 40 inches
Private Foundation, extended
loan, Georgia O'Keeffe Museum,
Santa Fe, New Mexico
CR 1082

68
Pedernal
1945
Pastel on paper
21 ½ x 43 ¼ inches
Georgia O'Keeffe Museum,
Santa Fe, New Mexico, Gift of
The Burnett Foundation
CR 1117

Seen from an Airplane

69
Another Drawing Similar Shape
1959
Charcoal on paper
24 ⅞ x 18 ⅝ inches
Milwaukee Art Museum,
Milwaukee, Wisconsin, Gift of
Jane Bradley Pettit Foundation
and The Georgia O'Keeffe
Foundation
CR 1341

70
Drawing V
1959
Charcoal on paper
24 ½ x 18 ¾ inches
Georgia O'Keeffe Museum,
Santa Fe, New Mexico, Gift of
The Burnett Foundation and The
Georgia O'Keeffe Foundation
CR 1339

71
It Was Yellow and Pink III
1960
Oil on canvas
40 x 30 inches
The Art Institute of Chicago,
Alfred Stieglitz Collection,
Bequest of Georgia O'Keeffe
CR 1442

72
Sky with Flat White Cloud
1962
Oil on canvas
60 x 80 inches
National Gallery of Art,
Washington, DC, Alfred Stieglitz
Collection, Bequest of Georgia
O'Keeffe
CR 1473

73
Winter Road I
1963
Oil on canvas
22 x 18 inches
National Gallery of Art,
Washington, DC, Gift of The
Georgia O'Keeffe Foundation
CR 1477

Chronology

1887 November 15
Georgia Totto O'Keeffe born to Francis Calyxtus O'Keeffe and Ida Totto O'Keeffe at family dairy farm, near Sun Prairie, Wisconsin, the first girl and the second of seven children, including Francis Calyxtus (1885–1959), Ida Ten Eyck (1889–1961), Anita Natalie (1891–1985), Alexius Wyckoff (1892–1930), Catherine Blanche (1895–1987), and Claudia Ruth (1899–1984).

1905–1906 Fall 1905

attends School of The Art Institute of Chicago.

1907–1908
Fall–spring: attends Art Students League, New York. June 1908: awarded League's 1907–1908 Still Life Scholarship. Summer 1908: as scholarship winner, attends League's Outdoor School at Lake George, New York.

1908–11
Fall 1908: moves to Chicago to work as free-lance commercial artist. Around 1910: becomes ill with measles and moves to Charlottesville, Virginia, to live with mother, sisters, and brothers, who move there from Williamsburg sometime in 1909.

1912
Summer: attends drawing class at University of Virginia, Charlottesville, taught by Alon Bement, of Teachers College, Columbia University, New York. August: moves to Amarillo, Texas, as supervisor of drawing and penmanship in public schools; holds position through spring 1914.

1913 Summer
returns to Charlottesville to work as Bement's assistant at University of Virginia (and continues to teach there summers through 1916).

1914–15
Fall 1914: enrolls at Teachers College, Columbia University. Fall 1915: moves to Columbia, South Carolina, to teach art at Columbia College. October 1915: produces seminal series of charcoal abstractions; sends examples to her friend in New York, Anita Pollitzer.

1916
January: Pollitzer takes O'Keeffe's drawings to Alfred Stieglitz at 291 gallery in New York on New Year's Day. March: O'Keeffe returns to Teachers College. May 1: mother dies in Charlottesville; attends funeral following day. May 23: Stieglitz opens group show at 291 that includes ten O'Keeffe charcoal drawings. June: O'Keeffe in Virginia to teach with Bement. Late August: moves to Texas to teach at West Texas State Normal College, Canyon. Stieglitz includes O'Keeffe work in group show at 291.

1917 April
Stieglitz opens "Georgia O'Keeffe," first one-person show of her work, at 291.

1918
Late February: O'Keeffe takes leave of absence from teaching and moves to Texas. June 10: moves to New York. July 8: Stieglitz leaves Emmeline Obermeyer Stieglitz, his wife since 1893, to live with O'Keeffe. O'Keeffe resigns from West Texas State, accepting Stieglitz's offer to underwrite a year of painting. November 11: O'Keeffe's father dies in Petersburg, Virginia.

1919
O'Keeffe and Stieglitz spend summer and fall at Lake George (a pattern that continues until 1929, when O'Keeffe starts working part of nearly every subsequent year in New Mexico).

1920
March: makes first of many trips to York Beach, Maine. December: in New York, O'Keeffe and Stieglitz move into house of Stieglitz's brother, Leopold, at 60 East 65th Street and live there winters through 1924.

1921 February
Stieglitz retrospective exhibition opens at The Anderson Galleries, New York; several nudes within the forty-five photographs of O'Keeffe create sensation.

1923 January
Stieglitz opens "Alfred Stieglitz Presents One Hundred Pictures: Oils, Water-colors, Pastels, Drawings, by Georgia O'Keeffe, American" at The Anderson Galleries.

1924
March: Stieglitz opens "Alfred Stieglitz Presents Fifty-One Recent Pictures: Oils, Water-colors, Pastels, Drawings, by Georgia O'Keeffe, American," at The Anderson Galleries. Spring: Stieglitz has kidney stone attack. September 9: Stieglitz's divorce finalized. November: O'Keeffe and Stieglitz move to apartment at 35 East 58th Street and, on December 11, are married.

1925
March: Stieglitz opens "Alfred Stieglitz Presents Seven Americans: 159 Paintings, Photographs & Things, Recent & Never Before Publicly Shown, by Arthur G. Dove, Marsden Hartley, John Marin, Charles Demuth, Paul Strand, Georgia O'Keeffe, Alfred Stieglitz" at The Anderson Galleries. During run of exhibition and in June: Stieglitz suffers kidney problems. July: O'Keeffe ill from reaction to vaccination. Mid-November: O'Keeffe and Stieglitz move to the Shelton Hotel, on Lexington Avenue, living there until 1936, when they move to 405 East 54th Street. December: Stieglitz opens The Intimate Gallery in The Anderson Galleries building.

1926
February: Stieglitz opens "Fifty Recent Paintings, by Georgia O'Keeffe," at The Intimate Gallery. Late February: O'Keeffe travels to Washington, DC, and speaks at National Woman's Party dinner. (She joins NWP in teens and maintains her membership until dissolution of party in 1970s.) April: travels to Cos Cob, Connecticut. June: Stieglitz hospitalized with severe kidney attack.

1927
January: Stieglitz opens "Georgia O'Keeffe: Paintings, 1926," at The Intimate Gallery. June: O'Keeffe has first of two breast surgeries for benign cyst removal. June: first retrospective, "Paintings by Georgia O'Keeffe," opens at The Brooklyn Museum. December: O'Keeffe has second surgery.

1928

January: Stieglitz opens "O'Keeffe Exhibition," at The Intimate Gallery. Mid-September: Stieglitz has first severe angina attack, O'Keeffe spends weeks nursing him.

1929

February: Stieglitz opens "Georgia O'Keeffe: Paintings, 1928," at The Intimate Gallery. April 27: O'Keeffe and artist Rebecca Strand (wife of Paul Strand) go to Santa Fe, New Mexico, then to Taos as guests of arts supporter-writer Mabel Dodge Luhan, who provides O'Keeffe a studio; O'Keeffe learns to drive and purchases automobile. August 25: leaves for Lake George via Chicago. December 13: "Paintings by 19 Living Americans," with five works by O'Keeffe, opens at Museum of Modern Art, New York. December 15: Stieglitz opens final gallery, An American Place.

1930

February: Stieglitz opens "Georgia O'Keeffe: 27 New Paintings, New Mexico, New York, Lake George, Etc.," at An American Place. June: O'Keeffe goes to New Mexico, returning in September to New York.

1931 Late April

O'Keeffe to New Mexico, returning in July to Lake George. December 27: Stieglitz opens "Georgia O'Keeffe: 33 New Paintings (New Mexico)" at An American Place.

1932

May–October: back and forth between Lake George and New York; in June and in August, travels to Canada. In October, stops painting entirely.

1933

January: Stieglitz opens "Georgia O'Keeffe: Paintings – New & Some Old," at An American Place. February: O'Keeffe hospitalized for psychoneurosis. March through April: recuperates in Bermuda. May–December: O'Keeffe at Lake George with occasional trips to New York.

1934

January–February: at Lake George; resumes painting after thirteen-month hiatus; Stieglitz opens "Georgia O'Keeffe at 'An American Place,' 44 Selected Paintings 1915–1927." March–April: O'Keeffe travels to Bermuda. June: travels to Chicago and New Mexico.

1935

January: Stieglitz opens "Georgia O'Keeffe: Exhibition of Paintings (1919–1934)," at An American Place. March: O'Keeffe to Lake George. April: has appendectomy. May: vacations in Ogunquit, Maine. June: returns to Lake George. July: drives to New Mexico and back to New York in November.

1936

January: Stieglitz opens "Georgia O'Keeffe: Exhibition of Recent Paintings, 1935," at An American Place. April: O'Keeffe and Stieglitz move to penthouse at 405 East 54th Street. June: O'Keeffe spends first summer at Rancho de los Burros, the Ghost Ranch, New Mexico, house she buys in 1940. September: returns to New York.

1937

February: Stieglitz opens "Georgia O'Keeffe: New Paintings," An American Place, New York, N.Y." June: at Lake George. July: O'Keeffe leaves for New Mexico, returning in October to New York. December: Stieglitz opens "Georgia O'Keeffe: The 14th Annual Exhibition of Paintings with Some Recent O'Keeffe Letters," at An American Place.

1939

January: Stieglitz opens "Georgia O'Keeffe: Exhibition of Oils And Pastels," at An American Place. Late January–April: O'Keeffe travels to Hawaii.

1940

February: Stieglitz opens "Georgia O'Keeffe: Exhibition of Oils and Pastels," at An American Place. February–March: O'Keeffe travels to Nassau. June: travels to New Mexico. October: buys Ghost Ranch house. December: discovers Abiquiu property that she will purchase in 1945; returns to New York.

1941

January: Stieglitz opens "Exhibition of Georgia O'Keeffe," at An American Place. May: O'Keeffe travels to New Mexico, returning in November to New York.

1942

February: Stieglitz opens "Georgia O'Keeffe: Exhibition of Recent Paintings, 1941," at An American Place. June: O'Keeffe travels to New Mexico, returning in December to New York; moves with Stieglitz to 59 East 54th Street, her last New York address.

1943

January: O'Keeffe travels to Chicago to install and attend retrospective, "Georgia O'Keeffe," at Art Institute of Chicago, organized by Daniel Catton Rich. March: Stieglitz opens "Georgia O'Keeffe: Paintings – 1942–1943," at An American Place. April: O'Keeffe goes to New Mexico, returning in October to New York.

1944

January: Stieglitz opens "Georgia O'Keeffe: Paintings – 1943," at An American Place. April: O'Keeffe travels to New Mexico; Rosalind Irvine, secretary of the American Art Research Council at the Whitney Museum of American Art, approaches Stieglitz about a catalogue of O'Keeffe's work. September: O'Keeffe returns to New York.

1945

January: Stieglitz opens "Georgia O'Keeffe: Paintings, 1944," at An American Place. May: O'Keeffe travels to New Mexico via Chicago, returning in November to New York. December: purchases Abiquiu property from Catholic Archdiocese of Santa Fe.

1946

February: Stieglitz opens "Georgia O'Keeffe," at An American Place. Begins working with Irvine on catalogue of her work. June: O'Keeffe travels to New Mexico. July 10: Stieglitz is found unconscious from a stroke; O'Keeffe returns to New York. July 13: Stieglitz dies. Late September: O'Keeffe returns to New Mexico. Fall: employs Doris Bry to help organize the Stieglitz papers; begins correspondence with Edith Halpert, owner of The Downtown Gallery, who becomes O'Keeffe's exclusive agent in 1950. December: O'Keeffe returns to New York.

1947 January through early summer

O'Keeffe in New York (where she primarily lives until 1949), working with Bry to settle the Stieglitz Estate.

1949 June

settles permanently in New Mexico, spending winter and spring in Abiquiu and summer and fall at Ghost Ranch.

1950 January and August

in New Mexico, Bry uses records of O'Keeffe's work established by O'Keeffe and Rosalind Irvine between 1946 and 1950, to begin compiling Abiquiu Notebooks, O'Keeffe's personal inventory of her work.

1951 September

proposes "O'Keeffe Paintings in Pastel: 1914–1952" to Halpert (opens in February 1952).

1958 February

travels to New York to install "Georgia O'Keeffe: Watercolors, 1916–17," at The Downtown Gallery.

1960 July

O'Keeffe and Bry help Daniel Catton Rich organize retrospective, "Georgia O'Keeffe: Forty Years of Her Art," for the Worcester Art Museum, Worcester, Massachusetts.

1963 August

severs relationship with Halpert and appoints Bry as agent.

1966

March: attends opening of retrospective, "Georgia O'Keeffe: An Exhibition of the Work of the Artist from 1915 to 1966," at the Amon Carter Museum of Western Art, Fort Worth, Texas. August: receives Wisconsin Governor's Award for Creativity in the Arts.

1968

During year, O'Keeffe's eyesight begins to fail.

1970 Early October

installs retrospective, "Georgia O'Keeffe," at Whitney Museum of American Art, New York, which opens on October 8.

1972

During year, suffers onset of macular degeneration and completes last unassisted oil painting, though works in oil with assistance until 1977 (works unassisted in watercolor and charcoal until 1978 and in graphite until 1984).

1973 November

meets potter-sculptor Juan Hamilton, who becomes her assistant and, later, her close friend, traveling companion, and facilitator, making possible completion of several projects.

1974

Spring and summer: completes text for *Some Memories of Drawings*. October: Hamilton begins teaching O'Keeffe to work with clay, which she explores through 1985. Receives New Mexico's First Annual Governor's Award.

1976

During year, Viking publishes *Georgia O'Keeffe*.

1977

Spring: dismisses Bry as agent. November: Perry Miller Adato video premieres on television.

1984

O'Keeffe moves, with Hamilton and family, to large house in Santa Fe, Sol y Sombra, to be nearer medical facilities.

1986 March 6

O'Keeffe dies in Santa Fe; her will names Hamilton its major beneficiary; will contested by O'Keeffe's surviving sister, Catherine Klenert, and Alexius O'Keeffe's daughter, June Sebring.

1987

Catherine Klenert dies. Late January: O'Keeffe's will settled, providing distribution of assets and formation of a foundation.

1989 July

The Georgia O'Keeffe Foundation is established to perpetuate the artistic legacy of the artist.

1991 September

O'Keeffe Foundation and National Gallery of Art sponsor project to produce first catalogue raisonné of the artist's work.

1997 July

Georgia O'Keeffe Museum, Santa Fe, founded by Anne and John Marion, opens; announces plans for Georgia O'Keeffe Museum Research Center in Santa Fe.

1998

August: Abiquiu House designated National Historic Landmark. July: Hamilton and wife, Anna Marie, announce donation of O'Keeffe's personal property (studio materials, library at Ghost Ranch, and found objects frequently depicted in her art) to O'Keeffe Museum Research Center; September: O'Keeffe's Ghost Ranch House acquired for Georgia O'Keeffe Museum and Research Center by The Burnett Foundation.

1999 December

Publication of Barbara Buhler Lynes, *Georgia O'Keeffe: Catalogue Raisonné* (London and New Haven: Yale University Press).

Selected References

1943

Flint, Ralph. "Lily Lady Goes West." *Town & Country* 98 (January 1943), pp. 34, 64–65.

1945

"Money Is Not Enough." *Time* 45 (February 5, 1945), p. 86.

1960

Worcester, Massachusetts, Worcester Museum of Art. *Georgia O'Keeffe – Forty Years of Her Art.* Text by Daniel Catton Rich. Worcester, 1960.

Kuh, Katharine. *The Artist's Voice: Talks with Seventeen Artists.* New York: Harper & Row, 1962.

1966

Fort Worth, Texas, Amon Carter Museum of Western Art. *Georgia O'Keeffe: An Exhibition of the work of the Artist from 1915 to 1966.* Ed. Mitchell A. Wilder. Fort Worth, 1966.

1970

New York, Whitney Museum of American Art. *Georgia O'Keeffe.* Text by Lloyd Goodrich and Doris Bry. New York: Praeger, 1970.

1971

Forman, Nessa. "Georgia O'Keeffe and Her Art: 'Paint What's in Your Head.'" *Philadelphia Museum Bulletin*, October 22, 1971.

1973

Chicago, Judy, and Miriam Schapiro. "Female Imagery." *Womanspace Journal* 1 (Summer 1973), pp. 11, 13.

1974

O'Keeffe, Georgia. *Some Memories of Drawings.* Intro. by Doris Bry. New York: Atlantis Editions, 1974.

Tomkins, Calvin. "Profiles: The Rose in the Eye Looked Pretty Fine." *The New Yorker* 50 (March 4, 1974), pp. 40–66.

1975

Chicago, Judy. *Through the Flower: My Struggle as a Woman Artist.* Garden City, New York: Doubleday & Co., 1975.

1976

Lippard, Lucy. *From the Center: Feminist Essays on Women's Art.* New York: E.P. Dutton, 1976.

O'Keeffe, Georgia. *Georgia O'Keeffe.* New York: The Viking Press, 1976; New York: Penguin Books, 1985.

Schwartz, Sanford. "When New York Went to New Mexico." *Art in America* 64 (July/August 1976), pp. 93–97.

1977

Adato, Perry Miller (producer and director). *Georgia O'Keeffe.* Videotape, 59 min. Produced by WNET/THIRTEEN for Women in Art, 1977. Portrait of an Artist, no. 1. Series distributed by Films, Inc./Home Vision, New York.

Kotz, Mary Lynn. "Georgia O'Keeffe at 90: 'Filling a Space in a Beautiful Way. That's What Art Means To Me.'" *Art News* 76 (December 1977), pp. 36–45.

Rose, Barbara. "O'Keeffe's Trail." *New York Review of Books* 24 (March 31, 1977), pp. 29–33.

1986

New York, Hirschl & Adler Galleries. *Georgia O'Keeffe: Selected Paintings and Works on Paper.* Intro. by Robert Pincus-Witten. New York, 1986.

1987

Peters, Sarah Whitaker. *Becoming O'Keeffe: The Early Years.* New York: Abbeville Press, 1991.

1989

Lynes, Barbara Buhler. *O'Keeffe, Stieglitz and the Critics, 1916–1929.* Ann Arbor: UMI Research Press 1989; reprint Chicago: University of Chicago Press, 1991.

1999

Lynes, Barbara Buhler. *Georgia O'Keeffe: Catalogue Raisonné.* London and New Haven: Yale University Press, The National Gallery of Art, The Georgia O'Keeffe Foundation, 1999.

2000

Fine, Ruth E., Barbara Buhler Lynes, Elizabeth E. Glassman, and Judith Walsh. *O'Keeffe on Paper.* New York: Harry N. Abrams, 2000.

2001

Messinger, Lisa Mintz. *Georgia O'Keeffe.* (World of Art series). London and New York: Thames & Hudson, 2001.

Index of Works of Art